T5-BPY-306

Withdrawn from
Davidson College Library

Library of
Davidson College

EDUCATION IN BRAZIL

World Education Series

The Soviet Union
Education in Scotland
Education in East Germany
Education in New Zealand
Education in Canada
Education in Australia
Education in Venezuela

World Education Series

Education in Brazil

FAY HAUSSMAN

Institut International
d'Etudes sur l'Education

and

JERRY HAAR

U.S. Department of
Health, Education, and Welfare

ARCHON BOOKS

1978

For Lorraine and Claude

For my parents Albert and Selma Haar

© Fay Haussman and Jerry Haar 1978
All rights reserved. No part of this publication may be reproduced, stored in a retrieval system, or transmitted, in any form or by any means, electronic, mechanical, photocopying, recording or otherwise, without the permission of the publisher

370.981
H377e

First published 1978 as an Archon Book, an imprint of The Shoe String Press Inc, Hamden, Connecticut 06514

Library of Congress Cataloging in Publication Data

Haussman, Fay
Education in Brazil.

(World education series)
Bibliography: p.
Includes index.
1. Education—Brazil. I. Haar, Jerry – joint author.
II. Title.
LA556.H34 370'.981 77-17797
ISBN 0-208-01705-4

Printed in the United States of America

78-5887

Contents

List of Tables

Acknowledgments

It is not possible to list here all those individuals who willingly furnished their time and materials to aid us in undertaking this project.

We would like, however, to acknowledge our gratitude to those persons whose assistance was truly indispensable in completing this book. They are: Jaroslav V. Zich, Director of the Institut International d'Etudes sur l'Education, Brussels; John W. F. Dulles, University of Texas; James Cass, Education Editor of *Saturday Review*; Richard Duncan, U.S. Agency for International Development; Frank M. Tiller, University of Houston; Eurides Britto, formerly with the Brazilian Ministry of Education and Culture (MEC); MEC officials Raul Romero de Oliveira and Newton Sucupira; and Cecilia Malizia Alves, librarian at the Pontifical Catholic University of Rio de Janeiro.

We are also grateful for the permission of *Saturday Review*, *The Times Educational Supplement*, and *The Times Higher Education Supplement* to use material from articles by the author previously published.

Foreword

WE have two main reasons for this study. The first one is the lack of any up-to-date reference work on Brazilian education. Events in Brazil in the last fifteen years have spawned a staggering number of studies. Most of them were written by U.S. academics whose preeminence as Brazilianists has, incidentally, been both acclaimed and deplored by Brazilian intellectuals. Political scientists, historians, and sociologists have tried to document, explain, and analyze the events leading up to Brazil's military coup of 1964, as well as its consequences. Economists have grappled with the phenomenon of what has become known as Brazil's 'economic miracle,' the sharp, upswing in Brazil's economy starting in 1967. Anyone interested in recent political or economic changes in Brazil can thus consult a wide range of up-to-date writings. In contrast, recent developments in Brazilian education have so far remained practically undocumented.

Educational research by Brazilian and U.S. specialists in the last few years has as a rule focused on specific aspects of different pedagogic areas, and has related to developments in Brazilian education as a result of the 1961 Law of Bases and Directives, Brazil's first general education law. That law, however, with the Basic Education Law of 1971 has undergone far-reaching modifications barely ten years later.

This study is, so far as we know, the first attempt to give a comprehensive overview of Brazilian education after 1971.

Our second reason for undertaking to write this study is that we found ourselves to be particularly well informed and thought we could do justice to a generally neglected subject. Both of us have closely observed the Brazilian educational panorama for a number of years. The material for this study was collected by Fay Haussman during her many trips all over the country to gather material for her education articles, and by Jerry Haar while he worked in Brazil on his doctoral thesis.

We would like this study to serve as a basic reference work for academics as well as nonacademics with a variety of interests. Academics may find it useful as a springboard for future studies and analyses of one or the other multifaceted and, inevitably, controversial topics presented here. Nonacademics, by which we mean anyone at all interested in events in Brazil, may find this concise and, we hope, easily intelligible text useful to complement the available information on other Brazilian phenomena. But since, as already said, so much of that information is so richly and so easily available, we have limited this text as far as possible to education alone. Political, economic, and social questions have been dealt with only marginally. We also think that it would be far too early to attempt a critical evaluation of Brazilian education after 1971, within a wider political, social, and economic framework, simply because so much of the recent reform still remains to be implemented.

We know that we saw Brazilian education in an upswing, propelled in tandem by social pressures and economic needs. We would, however, not venture to predict how far that upswing will go, let alone conclude that the millennium has finally arrived for this historically neglected sector of Brazilian development.

Serious and sustained concern for universal education in Brazil is less than fifty years old. It is, however, far from fortuitous that even as Brazilian education expanded it should have continued to perpetuate the standards of a traditionally stratified society. Brazilians writing about their education system often qualify it as being 'somnolent' and 'morose.' By this they mean that Brazilian education has failed to keep step with the demands of a changing society. The fact is that Brazilian education has remained remarkably attuned to the *true* demands of that society's most influential sectors. Educational opportunities massified or, as is often said, exploded in the last four decades, but in spite of consecutive 'reforms' the expanding educational system remained essentially rigid, selective, elitist, and overwhelmingly academic. It thus provided for society's needs without altering its hierarchic structure. Brazil has had the disadvantage of clinging to an aristocratic tradition of education for social prestige long after that tradition became archaic, and indeed counterproductive.

One of Brazil's chief problems may be—and that problem does not limit itself to education—that it seems to have leapfrogged from the eighteenth century straight into the twentieth. In the United States primary education became universal and compulsory in the nineteenth century, as a corollary of the industrial revolution and the continuing sweep of social and democratic ideals. This led in the twentieth century to the expansion of universal education up to the secondary level, thus raising the educational level for all. Brazilians are still struggling with the endeavor of making basic education available to all of the nation's schoolage children, and to reshape outdated educational contents and methods to meet social needs.

The 1971 law, whose intent, effects, and potential are being shown in this study, was meant to reform Brazilian education by redefining its functions and goals. Brazilian skeptics say that this is merely another one of Brazil's periodic 'reforms' and, like them, doomed to fizzle into futility. Its serious critics claim that it has by far preceded the social, economic and political conditions indispensable for its implementation. They could be countered with the argument that among the chief hurdles to genuine educational change are the social sectors opposing it—or, in Brazil, so far reluctant to accept it.

In the long run, the successful implementation of educational change in Brazil will unquestionably depend on a multitude of extra-educational factors. To simplify an excruciatingly complex problem, one can only say that it will take far more than merely a greater number of better schools to remedy the structural shortcomings of a society whose least privileged children are forced to drop out of school before completing fourth grade.

But one could also say that in education, at least, the attempt has finally been made to project for equitable social development. In the last fifty years, Brazilian education has gyrated between massive, but still inadequate, numerical expansions, and technical, but socially irrelevant, pedagogic reformulations. For the first time in Brazil's educational history, the reform has harnessed the techniques of educational planning, and has involved technocrats, educators, humanists, politicians, and economists in its projection and, inevitably, in the unabated controversy accompanying its hesitant progress.

F.H.
J.H.

Abbreviations

ABE—Brazilian Educational Association
ARENA—National Renovating Alliance
CAI—Commission on International Affairs
CAPES—Office of Coordination for the Improvement of Higher Education Personnel
CFC—Federal Cultural Council
CFE—Federal Education Council
CINCRUTAC—Commission for the Promotion of Rural University Centers for Training and Community Action
CJ—Judicial Advisory Board
CND—National Council on Sports
CNMG—National Commission on Morals and Citizenship
CNPq—National Council of Scientific and Technological Development
CNSS—National Council on Social Service
CPI—Parliamentary Investigation Commission
CRUTAC—Rural University Centers for Training and Community Action
DA—Academic Directorate; also, Department of Administration
DAC—Department of Cultural Affairs
DAE—Department of Student Assistance
DAU—Department of University Affairs
DCE—Central Student Directorate
DED—Department of Sport and Physical Education
DEF—Department of Elementary Education

DEM—Department of Middle Level Education
DOD—Department of Documentation and Dissemination
DP—Department of Personnel
DSI—Division of Security and Information
DSU—Department of Supplemental Instruction
FCBTVE—Brazilian Foundation Center for Educational Television
FGV—Getúlio Vargas Foundation
FMTE—Maranhense Educational Television Foundation
FNDE—National Fund for Educational Development
FUNTEC—National Fund for Scientific and Technological Development
GOT—'Work-oriented' lower middle-level schools
IBGE—Brazilian Institute of Geography and Statistics
IGF—Inspector General of Finances
IME—Military Institute of Engineering
INEPE—National Institute of Educational Studies and Research
INL—National Book Institute
INPA—National Institute for Amazonian Research
INPE—Institute of Space Research
IPEA—Institute of Economic and Social Planning
ITA—Air Force Technological Institute
LDB—Law of Directives and Bases of National Education
MDB—Brazilian Democratic Movement
MEB—Basic Education Movement
MEC—Ministry of Education and Culture
MOBRAL—Brazilian Literacy Movement
NAEA—Nucleus of Postgraduate Amazonian Studies
PIPMO—Intensive Manpower Training Program
PUC—Pontifical Catholic University
SACI—Advanced System of Interdisciplinary Communications
SEA—Secretariat of Administrative Assistance
SEEC—Service for Educational and Cultural Statistics
SEG—General Secretariat
SENAC—National Commercial Training Service

SENAI—National Industrial Training Service
SENAR—National Service for Professional Rural Training
TVE-MG—Educational Television-Minas Gerais
UFRJ—Federal University of Rio de Janeiro
UFRN—Federal University of Rio Grande do Norte
UnB—University of Brasília
USP—University of São Paulo

VENEZUELA
COLOMBIA
PERU
BOLIVIA
PARAGUAY
ARGENTINE
URUGUAY
GUYANA
SURINAME
FRENCH GUYANA
ATLANTIC OCEAN
ATLANTIC OCEAN
RORAIMA
BOA VISTA
AMAPÁ
MACAPÁ
AMAZONAS
MANAUS
PARÁ
BELÉM
ACRE
RIO BRANCO
RONDÔNIA
RONDÔNIA
MATO GROSSO
CUIABÁ
MARANHÃO
SÃO LUÍS
PIAUÍ
TERESINA
CEARÁ
FORTALEZA
RIO GRANDE DO NORTE
NATAL
PARAÍBA
JOÃO PESSOA
PERNAMBUCO
RECIFE
ALAGOAS
MACEIÓ
ARACAJU
BAHIA
SALVADOR
GOIÁS
DISTRITO FEDERAL
BRASÍLIA
GOIÂNIA
MINAS GERAIS
BELO HORIZONTE
ESPÍRITO SANTO
VITÓRIA
RIO DE JANEIRO
RIO DE JANEIRO
SÃO PAULO
SÃO PAULO
SANTOS
PARANÁ
CURITIBA
SANTA CATARINA
FLORIANÓPOLIS
RIO GRANDE DO SUL
PORTO ALEGRE
FERNANDO DE NORONHA
SEA TERRITORIAL LIMITS (200 MILES)
SEA TERRITORIAL LIMITS (200 MILES) shown

I

Brazil

THE pageantry of Rio's *carnaval*, samba, tan young beauties on Copacabana Beach, the Amazon jungle, and coffee. These are things one readily associates with Brazil.

However, the people and government of this immense nation of many contrasts are intent upon conveying a different image—one of change and modernization, economic growth, and emerging world power status.

Brazil is truly on the move, striving to achieve its national aspirations. Certainly, that country's educational system plays—and will continue to play—a prominent role in the process.

A synopsis of Brazilian geography, culture, society, and politics will aid in understanding that nation's educational system. John Gunther, Eugene Fodor, and others have written flowing prose on Brazil for tourists and armchair travellers alike; and there is no need to try to replicate their fine efforts here. Consequently, the following synopsis is 'cut and dry,' providing a brief overview for those who most likely already possess a good comprehension of Brazilian issues and concerns.

GEOGRAPHY

Brazil is a giant. It is the fifth largest country in the world, covering 3,286,470 square miles and exceeded in territorial extent only by the Soviet Union, Canada, China, and the United States. With over 108 million inhabitants and an annual population growth rate of about 2.8 percent, Brazil is the seventh most populous nation, behind China, India, the U.S.S.R., the U.S., Indonesia, and Japan.

The nation is organized into twenty-one states, four territories, and a Federal District. The states of Rio de Janeiro, São Paulo, Paraná, Minas Gerais, Santa Catarina, and Rio Grande do Sul—the Southeast and the South—are where 90 percent of the population live on less than 30 percent of the land. The most populated areas are cities on or near the coast, and population is particularly dense in squatter settlements (*favelas*) where the urban poor live.

The burgeoning metropolises of Rio de Janeiro and São Paulo are located in Southeast Brazil. This region is the agricultural and industrial heartland of Brazil. The land and climate in São Paulo State, the Paraíba Valley, and the south of Minas Gerais are especially suited for agricultural growth and development. Rich highlands are insulated by the Serra do Mar escarpment, and moist winds and frequent cloud cover retard the normally stifling temperatures of the tropics. These factors enhance the cultivation of a wide variety of crops. In addition to coffee (of which Brazil is the world's largest producer), this region is a major source of dairy and beef products, sugar cane, rice, cotton, and cereals.

The State of Minas Gerais ('General Mines') is rich in mineral deposits, gold, diamonds, and semiprecious stones. Manganese, iron ore, and base metals are mined here, as well. Most of the ore is processed at Usiminas, the steelworks located eighty miles east of Belo Horizonte. It is the largest steel mill in Latin America.

The State of Rio de Janeiro is a significant manufacturing center. However, despite light industry, commerce, and an active international port, Rio de Janeiro is vastly overshadowed by Metropolitan São Paulo. Situated on a plateau 2,500 feet above sea level, São Paulo is the financial and industrial capital of Brazil. With a population exceeding 8.5 million, it is the largest city in Latin America and the fastest growing city in the world. São Paulo is the principal center for the manufacture of consumer durables, pharmaceuticals, textiles, chemicals, automobiles, and industrial equipment. A vibrant, cosmopolitan city—often considered a cross between New York and Chicago—São Paulo is plagued with the same problems as other large metropolitan areas: air and noise pollution, high density of population, traffic congestion, an increasing crime rate, and a high cost of living.

Northeast Brazil is the chief source of sugar cane production, cotton, cacao, bananas, and oils. However, for the most part it is a hot, semiarid, economically depressed area. Outmoded, noncompetitive agricultural methods, drought and disease are prevalent in the sparsely populated lowland interior. Poor migrant workers flock to the crowded coastal cities where they encounter difficulties of all kinds and poverty far greater than they had imagined. Government efforts have been underway to bring economic and social assistance to Northeast Brazil.

The South, encompassing the States of Paraná, Santa Catarina, and Rio Grande do Sul, is a prosperous region. The terrain is made up of highlands and interior and coastal plains. The climate is mild with frost and snow not uncommon in the interior highlands. Small farms rather than plantations are the rule; and although coffee is grown in northern Paraná, the most abundantly cultivated crops are wheat, potatoes, and various grains. Spacious pasture land makes this region a major cattle and sheep raising area. Extensive forests provide lumber which is processed into building materials and paper products. The capitals and outlying areas of these three southern states are centers of commerce and light industry. Rio Grande do Sul manufactures shoes, handbags, and leather and suede products for both the national and international markets.

The Center West is made up of interior plateaus and plains. These rolling hills and tablelands, which include the States of Mato Grosso and Goiás, account for one-third of the nation's national territory; yet, this region is sparsely populated. Brasília, an architectural wonder and the capital of Brazil, is located on a high plateau in this area. Cattle ranching and commercial farming are the primary economic activities in this subtropical frontier land.

Finally, the vast but barely populated states and territories forming the North of Brazil—Pará, Amazonas, Acre, Amapá, Roraima, and Rondônia—account for about 40 percent of the national territory known as the Amazon Basin which encompasses the world's largest rain forest. Heat, humidity, and torrential seasonal rain storms are this equatorial area's salient features, and its chief inhabitants are a multitude of exotic animals, often deadly ones. There are small settlements along the waterways; however, despite efforts to construct a highway system and attempts to exploit, develop, and populate the region, the Amazon remains a resource of presumably gigantic if still not fully known potential.

CULTURE

The major ethnic groups which have shaped Brazilian culture are the Portuguese, Indians, and Africans. The original inhabitants of Brazil were Indians, representing the Tupi-Guarani, Arawak, and Carib linguistic groups. They were heterogeneous tribal peoples whose level of development was considerably below that of the Aztec, Inca, and Mayan civilizations. The Brazilian aborigines were nomads who fished, hunted, and practiced primitive agriculture. They were fierce warriors, and many tribes were cannibalistic.

The Portuguese settlers acquired a basic understanding of indigenous culture, thus enabling them to meet many of the challenges they found in the New World. They considered the natives barbarians, however, and exploited and persecuted them. Still, racial mixing between white colonists and Indians was common and widespread. From among their offspring came the *bandeirantes*—the rugged, adventurous pioneers who blazed the trails through the interior of Brazil.

The colonists relied heavily on the Indian population to do the agricultural work. However, during the middle of the sixteenth century, the Portuguese had to bring in slaves (mostly from West Africa) to fill the labor shortage. Although uprooted from their native lands and subjected to authoritarian domination in the New

World, the experience of African slaves in Brazil was significantly different from that of their brothers in North America. Most importantly, Brazilian slavery was not characterized by racial hatred and absolute segregation. In the shaping of Brazilian culture, the African functioned as the 'cook, nursemaid, the servant, the playmate, the story-teller, and the sexual partner of the European.'[1]

The impact of the African influence on the formation of Brazilian culture was far more significant than that of the Indian. In religion, cuisine, art, and music, African culture left its mark, being adopted and adapted by the dominant culture. This legacy has endured from colonization through the present time.

As mentioned, both the Indian and African populations were physically, culturally, and religiously diverse groups. Moreover, to some extent the same can be said of the Portuguese colonists. The influx of various ethnic groups into the kingdom of Portugal produced two principal racial groups: the first, tall and blond, fair-skinned and bellicose; the second, short and dark-haired, olive-skinned and passive.[2] Havighurst and Moreira point out that: 'The first group predominated in the aristocracy, the second formed the base of the middle and lower classes. From the former group came the conquerors who tamed the wilderness of Brazil; from the latter came the populators and the cultivators.'[3]

The Portuguese were an adaptable people, tolerant of other races (compared to other colonialists), and prone to racial mixing. Consequently, race and culture in Brazil are, indeed, different from the motherland, Portugual.

Although Portuguese, Indians, and Africans comprise the fundamental elements of Brazilian culture, many other nationalities have

---

[1] Charles Wagley, *An Introduction to Brazil* (New York: Columbia University Press, 1971), p. 21.

[2] Oliveira Viana, *Evolução do Povo Brasileiro*, 4ª edição (Rio de Janeiro, 1956), p. 125. Among the predominant groups were Goths, Iberians, Romans, Celts, and Semites.

[3] Robert J. Havighurst and J. Roberto Moreira, *Society and Education in Brazil* (Pittsburgh: University of Pittsburgh Press, 1965), p. 24.

immigrated to Brazil to transform the nation into a truly multicultural one.

Although non-Portuguese migration occurred as early as the turn of the nineteenth century, it was not until the 1850s that foreigners came to Brazil in significant numbers. The first waves of immigrants consisted, for the most part, of Germans who settled in the southern states of São Paulo, Paraná, Santa Catarina and Rio Grande do Sul. According to one source, before the Second World War European immigration accounted for approximately one-third of the population of Paraná, Santa Catarina, and Rio Grande do Sul.[4]

In addition to the Germans, Italians and other Mediterranean peoples migrated to Brazil in great numbers beginning in the late nineteenth century. Thereafter, Japanese, Arabs, and Slavs came to Brazil, also settling in the south of the country. The majority of immigrants, except for those from the Middle East, became involved in agricultural activities as farm workers, truck farmers, and small commercial farmers. Although some immigrants eventually acquired large land holdings, a substantial number moved to the cities—São Paulo, Curitiba, Florianopolis, and Porto Alegre—where they entered business, labor, and the professions.

The second major wave of immigration followed World War II; however, contrary to popular belief, this was less significant than the earlier influx of foreigners. Today, there are still many Europeans seeking entry into Brazil (particularly Spanish and Portuguese, owing to economic conditions in their native lands).

Immigrants have been vital to the formation of Brazilian social and economic life. Those from Europe, in particular, contributed to the initial formation of the new middle class—small farmers, craftsmen, technicians, and bureaucrats. In the southern states, European immigrants have preserved some of the customs and life styles of the Old World. Enclaves of Italians in Caxias, Rio

---

[4] Leo Waibel, 'European Colonization in Southern Brazil,' *Geographical Review*, XL (October 1950).

Grande do Sul; Poles and Russians in Paraná; and Germans in Blumenau and Joinville, Santa Catarina, have sought to preserve their ethnic heritage.

Nevertheless, among all the major immigrant groups in the post-war period—Portuguese, Spaniards, Italians, Germans, Japanese, Russians and Poles—there is the genuine feeling that they are first and foremost Brazilians. In short, in terms of race and ethnic groups, Brazil is a melting pot. Racial and ethnic integration and assimilation, in a climate of tolerance, have produced many positive results, one being that Brazilians of all colors, faiths, and national origins participate in all aspects and on all levels of national life.[5]

It has been eloquently stated that:

> Brazil attracts more and more immigrants, without questions concerning their ethnic and national origins, certain of its power to assimilate them to its Portuguese base, which is always being renewed by the thousands of Portuguese who enter the country annually. Not only is a continuous crossing of the races and national groups occurring in Brazil; more important there is a continual renovating process of acculturation and enculturation which brings the immigrant into the national body and at the same time gives the nation some of the qualities of the immigrant. This being so, Brazil deserves the name of an anthropocultural democracy *sui generis*, perhaps alone in the contemporary world.[6]

SOCIAL CLASS

Since the Second World War, Brazilian society has become increasingly more stratified. Industrialization, urbanization, and other forces of modernization have produced significant changes in the social structure.

---

[5] Brazil's President Ernesto Geisel serves as an excellent example of the degree of integration and openness in Brazilian society. He is the offspring of German immigrant parents and is a Lutheran who heads the world's largest Catholic country.

[6] Havighurst and Moreira, p. 35.

In actuality there are five social classes in Brazil:[7]

Upper Class: large landowners and the urban upper class;
Upper-Middle Class: medium-sized rural landowners and upper level professional and businessmen;
Lower-Middle Class: smaller rural property owners, public employees, small merchants and manufacturers, lower level professional men;
Upper Working Class: workers employed in factories, railways, public service, transportation and communication;
Lower Working Class: farm laborers and unskilled urban workers.

TABLE 1

EARNINGS AND PARTICIPATION IN TOTAL INCOME BY INCOME LEVEL

Classes of Monthly Income (in 1970 cruzeiros)	*Number of Persons*		*Percentage of the Total Income Groups*	
	1960	*1970*	*1960*	*1970*
Income below 98	4,899,932	7,452,929	25.2	28.6
Income between 99 and 154	3,318,008	5,707,926	17.1	21.9
Between 155 and 210	2,534,189	4,682,106	13.0	17.9
Between 211 and 280	2,955,074	1,580,858	15.2	6.1
Between 281 and 466	3,247,010	3,166,785	16.7	12.1
Between 467 and 934	1,776,356	2,167,000	9.1	8.3
Between 935 and 2,333	569,267	1,038,199	2.9	3.9
2,334 and above	104,585	283,940	0.5	1.1
Average Monthly Income	206	282		

Source: *Veja*, 'A renda dos brasileiros,' 7 June 1972. Based upon data from Albert Fishlow, 'Brazilian Size Distribution of Income,' *American Economic Review* 62 (May 1972): pp. 391–402, and Carlos Geraldo Langoni, *Distribuição da Renda e Desenvolvimento Econômico do Brasil* (Rio de Janeiro: Editora Expressão e Cultura, 1973).

[7] Ibid., p. 100.

Those who have benefited most from the intensive postwar development efforts have been the upper-middle class, lower-middle class, and upper working class. They have filled the many new positions which have come about in both the private and public sectors as a result of economic expansion.

The situation of the lower working class has deteriorated during the last decade: real wages have declined and the maldistribution of income has worsened. As shown in table 1, the gap between rich and poor has clearly widened.

The key variable in income distribution is *education*. As illustrated in table 2, the higher the level of instruction, the greater the income. It is apparent that Brazilian economic development differentiates people mainly by education.

TABLE 2

INCOME DISTRIBUTION ACCORDING TO SECTOR AND LEVEL OF EDUCATION

	Percent of the Economically Active Population[a]			*Monthly Income in 1970 Cruzeiros*		
	1960	*1970*	*Percentage Variation*	*1960*	*1970*	*Percentage Variation*
Sector						
Rural	46.56	40.05	−13.98	129	138	+ 7
Urban	53.44	59.95	+12.18	273	378	+38
Level of Education						
Illiterate	39.05	29.75	−23.81	111	112	—
Primary	51.71	54.47	+5.34	211	240	+14
Junior high (*ginásio*)	5.16	8.03	+55.62	440	482	+ 9
Senior high (*colégio*)	2.67	5.24	+96.25	536	688	+28
University	1.40	2.51	+79.28	1,123	1,706	+52

Source: Carlos Geraldo Langoni, *Distribuição da Renda e Desenvolvimento Economico do Brasil*, p. 86.

[a] Economically active population: in 1960, 19,404,421; in 1970, 26,079,743.

POLITICS

On March 31, a civilian-supported military coup d'état overthrew the democratically elected leftist government of President João Goulart. The armed forces' intervention was triggered by growing concern with rampant inflation, governmental corruption, and Communist infiltration.

Upon assuming power, the military swiftly moved to eradicate subversion and bring the spiraling inflation under control. Through a series of 'Institutional Acts,' political freedom was significantly curtailed, and the government assumed sweeping powers to act whenever and wherever it chose, in the name of 'national security.' The military dissolved Brazil's thirteen political parties in 1965 and abolished direct presidential elections. Two new political parties were authorized: the pro-government National Renovating Alliance (ARENA) and the opposition Brazilian Democratic Movement (MDB). Although the MDB had in essence been merely a token opposition, it came out of the November 1974 legislative elections, which admittedly had been the freest ever allowed by the military regime, with substantial and surprising gains: it won sixteen of twenty-two available Senate seats and almost one-half of the seats in the Chamber of Deputies. Concerned with this massive expression of popular dissatisfaction, the government passed a new law prior to the 1976 municipal elections, limiting television election propaganda and thus curtailing particularly the exposure of MDB candidates. In November 1976, ARENA won 3,179 mayoral contests as against 610 won by the MDB. The pro-government party also elected 25,730 councilmen; the MDB only 9,274. (It should be noted, however, that ARENA candidates ran unopposed in 1,789 of Brazil's 3,789 municipalities.) Although the election was a clear victory for ARENA, MDB won majorities in the largest cities of the nation: São Paulo, Rio de Janeiro, and Porto Alegre.

The Brazilian Constitution of 1969 (officially called 'Amendment No. 1' to the 1967 Constitution) incorporates all the amendments decreed by the military regime since 1964. The Constitution maintains the framework of legislative, executive, and judicial powers; however, mainly by incorporating Institutional Act No. 5 of December 1968, it delegates preponderant powers to the president, such as the power to cancel parliamentary mandates, to suspend political rights and, should he decide to decree a congressional recess, to legislate instead of Congress. The President is elected to a five-year term by members of Congress and delegates from the state legislatures.

The bicameral legislature, which functions today as little more than a rubber stamp, consists of the Senate and Chamber of Deputies; their members are elected by direct popular elections. The Senate is the upper house and is comprised of sixty-six members—three from each state, elected in rotation for eight-year terms. The country is divided into twenty-one states, three federal territories, and the Federal District (Brasília). There were twenty-two states until 1974, when the states of Guanabara and Rio de Janeiro were merged. After the 1978 elections, the Senate will have sixty-three members.

The Chamber of Deputies is the lower house where representation is proportionate to the number of voters. (All literate Brazilians over eighteen may vote.) In the 1974 elections, 364 Federal Deputies were elected for four-year terms.

This chapter has presented a brief overview of Brazilian geography, culture, society, and politics; the following chapters present and discuss the structure, administration, and function of Brazil's educational system.

2

Historical Development

THE COLONIAL SYSTEM OF EDUCATION*

THE Portuguese colonization of Brazil was aimed at short term exploitation rather than long term investment. Consequently, investment in education was not considered economically attractive. Even if popular education had been assigned a high priority, there were few major population centers and inadequate communications and transportation systems.

Brazilian society was predominantly agrarian, and education was reserved for members of the rural aristocracy. It was they who furnished the power elite for the State, the Church, and the professions. The education they received, however, was ornamental rather than functional—merely a social status symbol used to differentiate the upper class from the lower class.

The pattern of educational development in Brazil was shaped by social and economic organization in the colonies along with a great affinity with European culture, in general. Consequently, Brazilian education was classical in nature and elitist in orientation.

The strong influence of the Jesuits also contributed immeasurably to a humanist thrust in education. Arriving in Brazil in 1549 with the first Portuguese colonizers, the Jesuits were concerned at first with providing religious instruction and literacy training to the

* The historical sketch of Brazilian education found in Agnes E. Toward, 'Some Aspects of the Federal Education Council in the Brazilian Educational System' (Ph.D. dissertation, University of Texas, 1966), pp. 1–66, has been most helpful.

Indian children. Soon after, they offered a classical course of study to the upper class and studies to prepare clergymen in the colonies.

Jesuit instruction was dogmatic, authoritarian, and abstract. Rote learning and encyclopedism were also common features. An exclusive concern with literary and rhetorical studies merely enhanced the prestige of various members of the upper class; education did not serve as a means for upward social mobility, but instead perpetuated the elite cultural values of Brazilian colonial society.

After 200 years of cultural dominance, Jesuit influence was virtually ended in 1759 when Portuguese Prime Minister Pombal expelled them in an effort to reform the administrative system of Portugal. Pombal replaced the Jesuits with lay teachers, extended educational opportunities, centralized administration, and expanded the curriculum to include such subjects as physics, geometry, and design. Concurrently, classes known as *aulas régias* (regal courses) were created under the Portuguese crown to prepare public administrators and military officers.

Although Jesuit *colégios* (actually, high schools) existed in sixteenth-century Brazil, higher education did not emerge until 1808 when the Portuguese court fled to Brazil in anticipation of Napoleon's invasion of Portugal.

After 1808 and well into the middle of the nineteenth century, higher education remained exclusively professional in nature; offering study in such fields as medicine, surgery, economics, agriculture, chemistry, design, and mechanical drawing. The emphasis on professional studies represented a radical break with the scholasticism of the literary period (before the expulsion of the Jesuits) and strongly influenced the future development of higher education in Brazil.

EDUCATION DURING THE EMPIRE PERIOD

The colonial period ended in 1822 when Dom Pedro I declared Brazil's independence from Portugal. The Empire of Brazil was established and survived for almost seventy years.

Although the Constitution of 1824 guaranteed universal education as a civil right, a system of free public education did not come about, because of insufficient physical and human resources and a lack of public interest. The educational expansion which took place did not significantly affect the masses; the entire system of instruction was geared either to preparatory studies for admission to one of the professional schools or to advanced study in music, fine arts, and humanities.

The government did show concern about education during the Empire, principally through legislation. Undoubtedly, the most important educational law was the Additional Act of 1834. Primary and secondary education were decentralized, organizationally and administratively, with responsibility assigned to the provinces. Higher education was left to the federal government.

One cannot deny the achievement of educational advancement during the Empire period. The first normal school and official secondary school (Colégio Pedro II) were created; primary schools expanded; and several agricultural and vocational-technical schools were founded. Higher education expanded—however, only in the form of single purpose colleges: self-contained professional schools.

However, educational advancement continued to be of, by, and for the upper classes. (The illiteracy rate during the Empire period never fell below 85 percent.) The secondary schools still maintained the college preparatory arts and letters program of studies, reminiscent of colonial, Jesuit-administered education. As for education, it too was tied to the past. Even in the professional preparation of physicians and lawyers, the orientation was largely humanistic. (The only truly professional schools in Brazil before the late nineteenth century were those for military officers, engineers, and doctors.)

Throughout the Empire period and well into the twentieth century, the upper classes exerted their influence largely through the liberal professions of law and medicine—particularly the former. The law schools were elite training grounds, and a judicial mentality came to dominate Brazilian social and political institutions.

THE EARLY REPUBLICAN PERIOD

A politically liberal military-civilian coalition deposed the Emperor in 1889 and established a republic. While major changes were anticipated, they did not come about. Conservatism did give way to new attitudes and ideas about business and government; however, Brazil remained fundamentally a rural, elite-dominated nation. Only 5 percent of the population was eligible to vote, and an oligarchy continued to control the political system.

After 1920 the forces of modernization accelerated; industrialization, urbanization, and the genesis of a small middle class were major features of change. The social fabric of modern Brazilian society began to take shape during this period.

In spite of a growing middle class and much attention to the cultivation of democracy, legacies remained: a high rate of illiteracy; governance by a conservative, upper class minority; a persistent maldistribution of wealth, power, and influence; and a predilection for European culture, with its literary and humanistic core.

As for educational development, the Constitution of 1891 created a dual system of education—the responsibility divided between the states and the federal government. A system of primary, secondary, and higher education would be administered by the states while the federal government would be responsible for a federal system of secondary and higher education.

One of the major influences during this period was positivism. Minister of Education Benjamin Constant applied many of Auguste Comte's ideas to Brazilian education. Principally, the curriculum underwent a change by which sciences, mathematics, acquisition of information, and the development of skills were foremost concerns. The scientific method, criticism, and analysis were finally introduced into the system of instruction.

Primary education in Brazil emerged along two lines. One was the United States-influenced system of elementary education adopted in the State of São Paulo. Innovation, experimentation, and new teaching methods characterized the pioneering efforts of São Paulo. The other orientation which gained popularity in other states was the European, especially French, system of education.

In both cases, public education was situated for the most part in urban areas; the quality of education in the countryside was poor.

The federal education system made less progress than the states in educational development. The federal government was less responsive to progressive concepts and methods in its own system of instruction, preferring instead the structure and content of the past—namely, the Empire period. For example, secondary education was modeled after the French *lycée*. Classical subjects required were numerous and extremely rigorous; only the best survived academically, and not all these students gained admission to higher education.

Although higher education expanded during the early Republican period, it was still predominantly in the form of professional schools. Between 1890 and 1930 seventeen law schools, eight medical colleges, and eight engineering schools were inaugurated. Brazil's first university, the University of Rio de Janeiro, was not created until 1920. Seven years later, the University of Minas Gerais was dedicated. However, these 'universities' consisted of joining together several professional schools—law, medicine, engineering—and, therefore, did not constitute a modern university, as it is commonly understood.

None can deny that educational progress was made during the early Republican period. However, this progress fell short of meeting the educational needs of Brazilian economic development and providing social equality for the masses.

THE VARGAS ERA

Social and political discontent compounded by increasing economic disparity between the cities and the countryside led to the 1930 Revolution in which Getúlio Vargas came to power.

During the early Vargas period, public education grew in

importance. Innovative ideas of teaching and curriculum organization were discussed by members of the newly founded *Associação Brasileira de Educação* (ABE). The *Escola Nova* (New School) group was prominent in advocating the adoption of John Dewey's educational philosophy in which the school is recognized as a social and political vehicle for democratic change. Other groups were successful in persuading Vargas to channel resources into basic education to reduce the high rate of illiteracy.

Vargas's provisional government selected *Escola Nova* proponent Francisco Campos as minister of education and health, a new ministry created in 1930. One of Campos's major accomplishments was his 1931 law which altered secondary education by creating two cycles of schooling: one a five-year basic instructional cycle and the other a two-year preparatory course for professional study. The intention was to add a formative component to the college preparatory curriculum of secondary education. Minister Campos believed that Brazilian youth should receive more than preparation for higher education—they must be taught the proper habits, attitudes, and behavior to function as productive and responsible members of society. The educational provisions of the 1934 Constitution, in which governmental authority was further centralized, enabled the minister to implement his administrative policies.

As for higher education, Francisco Campos's 'Statute of Brazilian Universities,' decreed in April of 1931, established the concept of a university system and laid the ground work for its development. The decree stipulated that a 'university' consist of three faculties: law, engineering, and medicine; or the substitution of a faculty of education, sciences, and letters for one of the three. According to this criteria, Brazil's first university was the University of São Paulo founded in 1934.

Higher education grew very slowly. One of the reasons was the conflict between those who wanted to stress scientific research and the pursuit of knowledge for its own sake and those who advocated the primacy of professional education.

In 1937 President Vargas abolished Congress and set up a dictatorship. Vargas had played the extremists of the right against those of the left and capitalized on the citizenry's disillusionment with liberalism as the political path for Brazilians to follow. Consequently, many people gave tacit approval to the authoritarianism of Vargas's *Estado Nôvo* (New State).

The educational policies of the *Estado Nôvo* rejected the change, accommodation, and balance of the early Vargas era in favor of a short term solution to educational problems. The Deweyist philosophy of the *Escola Nova* became corrupted: all education was required to serve the objectives of the State. The real substantive problems of education were not addressed; instead, the foremost concerns centered on the political dimension of public education.

The expansion of education did take place; in fact, the 1937 Constitution cited the primacy of vocational education and universal primary schooling. Minister of Education Gustavo Campanema succeeded in reorganizing the Ministry of Education. Among other things, a pedagogical research institute was established and greater efficiency and coordination of administrative services were brought about. Campanema's 'Organic Law of Secondary Education,' formulated in 1942, attempted to modernize secondary schooling; however, it was, in fact, a step backwards—a highly authoritarian law which imposed an extremely rigid federal system of education upon all schools, private as well as public.

During the *Estado Nôvo*, quantity was substituted for quality in education; a homogeneous curriculum and rigid methods of instruction were introduced, and stop-gap measures were adopted to confront educational problems. This characterized all education, higher as well as primary and secondary.

THE POSTWAR DEMOCRATIC PERIOD

Vargas was overthrown after World War II, and a democratic republic was reestablished in 1946. Eurico Dutra, Vargas's minister of war, was elected president.

During the postwar period, the seeds of Brazilian economic growth began to sprout. Industrialization intensified, the employment rate increased, and public services expanded. Geographically, the cities benefited the most, and rural residents in great numbers began to migrate to urban areas in order to find good jobs. Not all economic indicators were positive ones, however. Galloping inflation and a widening income gap between rich and poor were serious problems which would plague Brazil for years to come.

In an effort to change the educational system to meet the needs of social and economic development, Minister of Education Clemente Mariani formed a commission in 1947 to develop a national education plan as authorized in the 1946 Constitution. Minister Mariani sought a long term and comprehensive educational plan which would complement other government efforts to modernize and decentralize social services. In 1948 a major education bill was submitted to Congress; however, it took thirteen years before becoming law: liberals and conservatives, private school and public school proponents, advocates of centralization and believers in decentralization intensely debated the bill's provisions.

The Law of Directives and Bases of National Education, known as the LDB, was both ambiguous and contradictory, watered down by numerous compromises and excessive revisions. It was only partially successful in its implementation.

Basically, the LDB once again decentralized education by setting up a dual system: federal and state. Although administration was decentralized on the local level, state and private schools remained under the vigilance of the federal government. The LDB centered principally on primary and secondary education; little attention was paid to higher education. Essentially, it modified the existing educational system; it did not create a new one.

The major deliberative body created by the 1961 law was the Federal Education Council. The Council monitored all levels of education, including higher education. The statutes and by-laws of colleges and universities were subject to approval by the federal government. The Federal Education Council was entrusted with setting the curriculum guidelines for all college degree programs in fields subject to licensing.

Brazilian higher education expanded dramatically during the postwar period. Universities grew from five in 1940 to thirty-two by 1961: twenty-two federally financed public institutions; six Roman Catholic; and one independent, nonsectarian institution. Enrollments increased from 21,000 in 1939 to 102,000 in 1961.

This then was the historical course of educational development in Brazil. From colonization through the early 1960s the most notable theme was the continual clash between the traditional institutions and attitudes of the colonial and imperial past and the contemporary forces of economic modernization and social democracy.

3
Legislation, Administration, and Finance

LEGISLATION

THE Brazilian Constitution establishes that education is a right of all, and that it is the duty of the State to provide education in the home and in the school. The Constitution specifies that the states and the Federal District will organize their own systems of education while the Union will be responsible for schooling in the remote federal territories and also provide education in a complementary manner anywhere necessary throughout Brazil. The Union has specific constitutional authority to legislate the 'directives and bases of national education.'

The seminal Law of Directives and Bases (No. 4,024) of 1961, Brazil's first general education law, modified the Brazilian educational system. The most profound feature of the law is the provision which decentralizes the educational system, organizationally and operationally. Within the framework of decentralization, the states have the freedom to organize their own systems of instruction.

The Law of Directives and Bases had been debated in Congress for thirteen years before its passage. However, it shortly became apparent that, in certain aspects, the law had become outmoded, particularly in light of the many changes which were taking place in Brazilian society as a result of economic and social development efforts. Consequently, a University Reform Law was promulgated

Davidson College Library

in 1968 which completely revoked the section of the Law of Directives and Bases pertaining to higher education.

Shortly thereafter, primary and secondary education underwent reform: Law No. 5,692 of 1971 established new directives and bases for first-level and second-level education.

The fundamental legislation which presently governs the Brazilian educational system consists of the following:

1. Law No. 4,024 of December 21, 1961, which defines the principles of national education and the general norms of organization. (However, sections pertaining to first-level, second-level, and higher education have since been superseded entirely.)
2. Law No. 5,540 of November 28, 1968, that specifies the norms for the structure and function of postsecondary education.
3. Decree-Law No. 464 of February 11, 1969, which complements Law No. 5,540.
4. Law No. 5,692 of August 11, 1971, which establishes the directives and bases of first-level and second-level education.

Within the framework set down in the fundamental legislation governing the directives and bases of national education, the states pass legislation governing their respective educational systems. It is the responsibility of the Federal Education Council, a normative and advisory body created by Law No. 4,024, to interpret educational legislation, to determine the directives of educational policy, and to issue the norms which regulate the different aspects of education such as curricular organization, authorization, and accreditation of postsecondary institutions.

Within their respective educational systems, the State Councils of Education also carry out similar normative functions (e.g., authorizing the establishment of postsecondary institutions). Although municipalities do not have their own educational systems, they can, however, pass laws concerning education—provided they respect the legislation dealing with directives and bases of national education and the fundamental law of the state system of which they are a part.

ADMINISTRATION

In Brazil, the administration of education is carried out on three levels: federal, state, and municipal. The fundamental characteristic of the three systems, from a legal-administrative standpoint, is that the activities of each are guided and coordinated by a normative body and directed by a central executive authority.

On the federal level, the responsibility for policy decisions, planning, and administration rests with the Ministry of Education and Culture (MEC). The supreme normative body is the Federal Education Council, linked directly to the MEC. The educational system of the states and the Federal District are organized in a similar way: a Secretary of Education and a State Education Council in each state are responsible for schooling. The composition of the State Education Councils and their specific powers (in addition to those outlined in federal laws) are established in the laws by which each state organizes its educational system. Municipalities can maintain educational institutions, and some of the more developed ones have a Secretariat of Education. As embodied in Law No. 5,692, municipalities do not constitute a separate system of education but rather are delegated any powers which the State Education Councils wish to confer upon them through Municipal Councils of Education (e.g., the selection of elective subjects as part of the curriculum).

The MEC monitors compliance with educational laws as well as decisions of the Federal Education Council. Thus it carries out a special role: the MEC is the ultimate administrative authority in the federal educational system and the agency responsible for the nation's educational policy—its formulation, execution, and evaluation.

The Federal Education Council has equally broad responsibilities within its own sphere of competence. In addition to its normative functions towards the federal education system, the Council is the ultimate normative authority for the national system of education—that is, *all* Brazilian education: private as well as public, secular as well as nonsecular. It defines the principles; sets the standards; and officially interprets, within the administrative sphere, all legislation pertaining to directives and bases. The State Education Councils must comply with the decisions of the Federal Council.

The Federal Education Council was created in 1961 by the Law of Directives and Bases and is composed of twenty-four leading educators, named by the president of Brazil, who serve for a term of six years. Every two years there is a turnover of one-third of the Council members. The Council consists of a Chamber of First-Level and Second-Level Education, a Chamber of Higher Education, and a Commission on Legislation. As the body officially responsible for interpreting education legislation, the Council judges the different cases submitted to it and elaborates upon educational law for the nation as a whole.

Although universities are theoretically autonomous—academically, administratively, and financially—they are, nevertheless, subject to the judicial authority of the Federal Education Council. Specifically, the statutes of universities must be approved by the Council, and the Council can curtail the autonomy of any university found in violation of legislation, statutory rules, or other regulations. The MEC has the authority to name, if need be, an acting rector for a university.

The authorization of isolated establishments of higher education (i.e. single-purpose colleges) maintained by states and municipalities is under the jurisdiction of the State Education Councils. The Federal Education Council, however, possesses the authority to accredit these institutions.

The MEC was created in 1930 as the Ministry of Education and Health. Over the years it had expanded haphazardly into a bureaucracy in which over seventy directors and chiefs were directly responsible to the Minister. Moreover, there was little, if any, consultation or coordination among the various organizational units.

In 1970, however, the Minister of Education and Culture decreed a complete administrative reform of the bureaucracy which gradually began to take effect in 1971. The reform was intended above all to rationalize administrative organization and it was rooted in the objectives of Brazilian educational policy and oriented towards the decentralization of the processes of execution. In this decentralized reform, the powers of central bodies were transferred to sector groups at the administrative level, to other levels of public administration, and from the public sector to the private sector. Another major aspect of the administrative reform was the simplification of the administrative structure by reducing the number of agencies and eliminating much of the duplication in the bureaucracy.

The basic organizational structure of the MEC is composed of the following (also see table 3):

1. Collective decision-making bodies and units of direct assistance to the Minister of Education:

- a. Federal Education Council
- b. Federal Cultural Council
- c. National Commission on Morals and Citizenship
- d. Commission for the Promotion of Rural University Centers for Training and Community Action
- e. Commission on International Affairs
- f. Cabinet
  - 1. National Council on Social Service
  - 2. National Council on Sports
- g. Judicial Advisory Board
- h. Division of Security and Information
- i. National Fund for Educational Development.

2. Central agencies of planning, coordination, and financial control:

- a. General Secretariat. The central unit responsible for planning, integration, programming, coordination, and evaluation
- b. Secretariat of Administrative Assistance. Responsible for planning and coordinating intermediate administrative support services

TABLE 3

BASIC ORGANIZATIONAL STRUCTURE OF THE MINISTRY OF EDUCATION AND CULTURE (MEC)

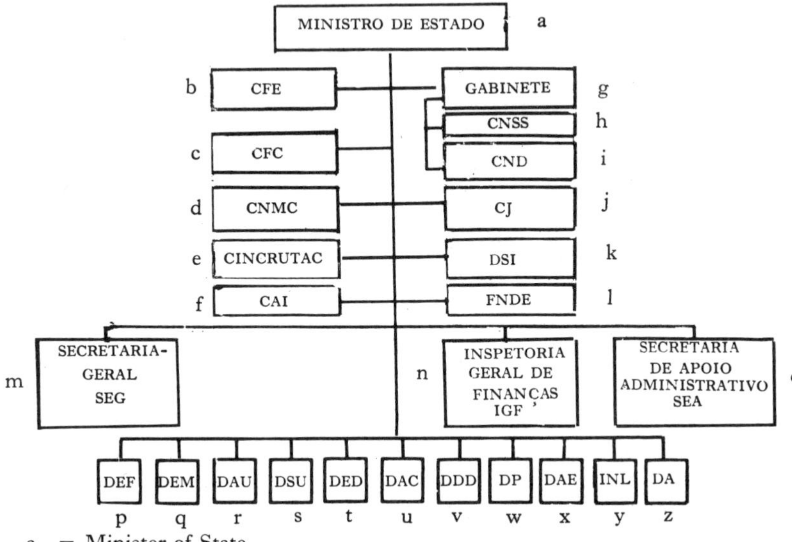

a = Minister of State
b = Federal Education Council
c = Federal Cultural Council
d = National Commission on Morals and Citizenship
e = Commission for the Promotion of Rural University Centers for Training and Community Action
f = Commission on International Affairs
g = Cabinet
h = National Council on Social Service
i = National Council on Sports
j = Judicial Advisory Board
k = Division of Security and Information
l = National Fund for Educational Development
m = General Secretariat
n = General Office of Finance (Office of the Inspector General)
o = Secretariat of Administrative Assistance
p = Department of Elementary Education
q = Department of Middle Level Education
r = Department of University Affairs
s = Department of Supplemental Instruction
t = Department of Sports and Physical Education
u = Department of Cultural Affairs
v = Department of Documentation and Dissemination
w = Department of Personnel
x = Department of Student Assistance
y = National Book Institute
z = Department of Administration

Source: MEC

c. General Office of Finance. Integrates the systems of administrative finance, accounting, and auditing, and cooperates with the general secretariat in monitoring the execution of programs and budgets.

3. Central organs under the direction of high level management which carry out the administration of specific activities and auxiliary services of the MEC. Such bodies are organized for the most part as departments. For example:

a. Department of Elementary Education (DEF), which is concerned with first-level schooling
b. Department of Middle Level Education (DEM), which is responsible for second level schooling
c. The Department of University Affairs (DAU), which is in charge of postsecondary education
d. The Department of Supplementary Education (DSU), which is responsible for adult education and all forms of schooling outside of formal school system
e. Department of Sports and Physical Education (DED)
f. Department of Cultural Affairs (DAC), which is responsible for all cultural activities.

Within the MEC there are a number of semiautonomous units such as the National Institute of Educational Studies and Research (INEPE) and the Office of Coordination of the Improvement of Higher Education Personnel (CAPES).

FINANCE

Education in Brazil is financed by both public and private funds. The sources of public sector expenditures are the federal government, the states, and the municipalities. With respect to private sources of support, a lack of reliable data makes it extremely difficult to determine with accuracy financial contributions to education of nonpublic sources of support. Nevertheless, it is estimated that in 1972 private sector expenditures as a whole

TABLE 4

TRENDS IN THE APPLICATION OF NATIONAL RESOURCES IN EDUCATION BY ADMINISTRATIVE SPHERE: 1970–75

Preliminary Figures (CR$ Millions)

YEAR	FEDERAL FUNDS			STATES & FED. DISTRICT			MUNICIPAL FUNDS			PRIVATE SECTOR			TOTAL	
	Curr. Prices	*Jan., 1975 Prices*	*Per-cent.*	*Curr. Prices*	*Jan., 1975 Prices*	*Per-cent*	*Curr. Prices*	*Jan., 1975 Prices*	*Per-cent*	*Curr. Prices*	*Jan., 1975 Prices*	*Per-cent*	*Curr. Prices*	*Jan., 1975 Prices*
1970	1,546	3,726	25.5	3,346	8,064	55.1	639	1,540	10.5	535	1,289	8.8	6,066	14,619
1971	2,071	4,183	24.4	4,541	9,173	53.5	871	1,759	10.3	999	2,018	11.8	8,482	17,134
1972	2,780	4,782	23.9	6,329	10,886	54.5	1,038	1,785	8.9	1,473	2,533	12.7	11,620	19,986
1973	3,737	5,531	23.6	8,695	12,869	54.8	1,172	1,734	7.4	2,249	3,328	14.2	15,853	23,462
1974	5,416	6,228	28.2	9,055	10,413	47.1	1,323	1,521	6.9	3,432	3,947	17.8	19,226	22,110
1975	7,639	7,639	27.0	13,879	13,879	49.1	1,494	1,494	5.3	5,232	5,232	18.5	28,249	28,249

SEG/MEC—1975

(1) Includes expenditures for all government programs, including general administrative expenditures, resources from other sources, and educational program expenditures of other ministries (including military); expenditures for science and technology are excluded.

(2) Budgetary data and estimate.

equaled 15 percent of public sector expenditures for national education (see table 4).

On the federal level, resources allocated for educational activities are not exclusively earmarked for the MEC. Several other ministries and government agencies develop and manage their own educational programs. For example, the Army maintains its own Military Institute of Engineering (IME) where, incidentally, the vast majority of students are civilians; the same is true for students of the Air Force Technological Institute (ITA). The Ministry of Planning also spends money in the area of education. Therefore the statistics cited in table 5 refer to *total* federal expenditures for education, not just those of the MEC.

TABLE 5

PUBLIC EXPENDITURES FOR EDUCATION: 1970–73
(1974 CR$ millions)

	SOURCE			
Year	*Federal*	*State*	*Municipal*	*Total*
1970	1,546	3,346	640	5,532
1971	1,858	4,541	919	7,318
1972	3,093	6,329	1,038	10,460
1973	3,991	8,735	1,172	13,898

Source: MEC

Public expenditures for education are presented in table 5. Public sources for educational expenditures are the following:

1. Ordinary resources from the National Treasury, the states, the Federal District, and municipalities. The collection and accounting of these resources are done without regard to final designation of the funds—that is, without a specific program in mind.

2. Resources for specific programs:
   a. *Salário-Educação*, instituted in 1964, is financed by a tax of the legal minimum monthly wage multiplied by the number of employees on the payroll of all private and public firms which contribute to Social Security. The collections from the *salário-educação* are $\frac{1}{3}$ from the federal government, on the one hand, and $\frac{2}{3}$ from the states and Federal District, on the other. The bulk of the funds are applied for programs of first-level education.
   b. Special Fund of the Federal Lottery, created in 1968, sets aside 20 percent of the total amount collected for education.
   c. The Federal Sports Lottery, created in 1969, contributes 30 percent of its revenues to education.
3. Resources from other sources:
   a. directly collected from decentralized administrative operations;
   b. collection of past-due monies;
   c. agreements with public and private entities;
   d. from other sources (public, private, and international).

Degree No. 66,254 of February 24, 1970, requires the states, the Federal District, federal territories, and municipalities to contribute annually a minimum of 20 percent of their share of the Participation Fund (*Fundo de Participação*) to first-level and second-level education programs. The Fund is derived from the general tax collections of the federal government; these monies are distributed to the various units of the federation in accordance with the principles established in the Brazilian Constitution. The federal decree defines the conditions for parceling out the amounts for education. The Constitution also permits the State to intervene when a municipality fails to make its yearly contribution to first-level education of at least 20 percent of its municipal tax receipts. In July 1975, Constitutional Amendment No. 5 was enacted, increasing the rate of federal revenue sharing in the Participation Fund.

In 1968, the government created the National Fund for Educational Development (FNDE) for the purpose of securing and coordinating resources and channeling them into the financing of education and research projects on all three educational levels, according to the directives of national educational planning. The Fund is administered by a decision-making council under the direction of the Ministry of Education and has at its disposal the following resources (1973 figures, based on 1974 cruzeiros):

1. Budgetary funds (CR$52,129,000,000)
2. Resources resulting from fiscal incentives (n.a.)
3. Twenty percent of the Special Fund of the Federal Lottery (3,000,000)
4. Thirty percent of the net receipts of the Sports Lottery (200,000,000)
5. Resources coming from the *salário-educação* (320,000,000)
6. Transfer payments by the Bank of Brazil, on the demand of the state governments, Federal District, and municipalities, as a matching contribution of financial assistance from the federal government (228,000,000)
7. Sums collected by the Brazilian government oil monopoly (PETROBRAS) for the purpose of financing teaching and research in geosciences (3,000,000)
8. Money received by the federal government as reimbursement for loans (143,000).

The National Fund for Educational Development also allocates monies from donations, inheritance taxes, and dividends on its bank accounts. Among its other responsibilities, the Fund finances federally sponsored programs (first-level, second-level, and higher education) and renders financial assistance to the states, Federal District, territories, municipalities, and private institutions. The financial assistance given is always contingent upon the approval of specific projects and programs and may or may not be reimburseable, depending upon the terms of the legal agreement reached by all parties concerned.

The Fund possesses relative administrative autonomy. Since it is not required to conform to strict rules in executing its budget, it has a great deal of financial flexibility.

After 1970, the Fund began to function effectively; and an increasing portion of resources (more than 75 percent in 1975) have been channeled to the MEC through the FNDE (see table 6).

TABLE 6

PERCENTAGE OF RESOURCES CHANNELED TO THE MEC THROUGH THE NATIONAL FUND FOR EDUCATIONAL DEVELOPMENT (FNDE)

Period	*MEC*	*FNDE*	*Percent*
1969	1,150,053,227.69	152,715,306.00	13.2
1970	1,337,094,189.29	169,351,927.50	12.6
1971	1,528,840,829.49	639,726,669.48	41.8
1972	2,242,362,258.68	906,602,112.09	40.4
1973	2,531,815,289.43	1,478,060,979.39	58.3
1974	2,901,331,900.00	2,287,927,800.00	78.4
1975 (+)	3,893,400,000.00	2,932,400,400.00	75.3

Source: FNDE/MEC/1975
(+) Preliminary Figures

A large part of the Fund's resources comes from the *salário-educação*, which explains why the largest portion of the Fund's disbursements goes to first-level schooling. However, while three-fourths of the *salário-educação* has been applied to first-level schooling in the past, the percentage contribution (although not the actual amount) has been declining, and in 1975 it equaled 48.5 percent (see table 7). (It should be mentioned that the Fund's disbursements are made primarily by means of financial assistance to the states.)

Constitutionally, since first-level and second-level schooling are the responsibility of the states and Federal District—the federal government fulfilling a supplemental role—educational outlays of the states and Federal District exceed those of the federal government. In 1975 this amounted to approximately 49.1 percent of the total national expenditures for education (a decline of 6 percent

TABLE 7

DISBURSEMENTS OF *Salário-Educação*: 1970–75

Year	*Funds*	*Dept. of Fundamental Ed.*	*Per-cent*	*Other Agencies*	*Per-cent*
1970	99,022,332.50	—	—	99,002,332.50	100.0
1971	126,214,804.31	97,105,942.59	76.9	29,108,861.72	23.1
1972	364,456,460.93	271,440,595.34	74.4	93,015,865.59	25.6
1973	392,216,156.82	244,746,455.78	62.4	147,469,094.04	37.6
1974	552,818,094.65	288,445,000.00	52.1	264,373,094.65	47.9
1975 (+)	722,085,100.00	350,300,000.00	48.5	371,785,100.00	51.5

Source: FNDE/MEC/1975
(+) Estimate

since 1970). The federal government's contribution, on the other hand, accounted for 27 percent of the nation's total educational outlays (an increase of 1.5 percent since 1970). (See table 4).

With respect to federal budgetary outlays for education, table 8 reveals that the trend during the first half-decade has been one of decline: as a percentage of the general budget of Brazil, federal education expenditures have declined from 3.1 percent in 1970 to 2.5 percent in 1975. However, it is important to note that some states spend 40 percent of their tax receipts on education. São Paulo State spends as much for education as the MEC itself!

TABLE 8

EDUCATIONAL EXPENDITURES IN PERCENTAGES OF THE FEDERAL BUDGET: 1970–1975

(*CR$ Millions*)

Year	*Federal Budget*		*Education*		*Percent*
	Current Prices	Jan. 1975 Prices	Current Prices	Jan. 1975 Prices	
1970	19,703	47,485	607	1,462	3.1
1971	26,739	54,012	848	1,713	3.2
1972	34,935	60,089	1,162	1,999	3.3
1973	52,129	77,151	1,585	2,436	3.0
1974	71,713	82,470	1,923	2,211	2.7
1975	113,396	113,396	2,875	2,825	2.5

Source: SG/MEC June 1975

Tables 9 and 10 note the steady yet modest percentage growth, as a ratio of the Gross Internal Product, in total educational expenditures (federal, state, municipal, and private), from 3 percent in 1970 to 3.6 percent in 1974. When one considers that the Gross Internal Product displays high indexes of growth beginning in 1968 (averaging 10 percent annually), the percentage increase in total educational outlays, indeed, represents a respectable increase in the amount of funds spent for education in Brazil.

TABLE 9

EDUCATION EXPENDITURES IN PERCENTAGES OF GROSS INTERNAL PRODUCT: 1970–75

Year	PUBLIC				TOTAL			
	Federal	*State & Municipal*	*Total*	*Private Sector*	*Current Prices*	*Jan. 1975 prices*	*US$ Jan. 1975*	*Percent*
1970	1,546	3,988	5,531	535	6,066	14,619	820	3.0
1971	2,071	5,412	7,483	999	8,482	17,134	1,146	3.0
1972	2,780	7,367	10,147	1,473	11,620	19,985	1,571	3.3
1973	3,737	9,867	13,604	2,249	15,853	23,462	2,143	3.4
1974	5,416	10,378	15,794	3,432	19,226	22,110	2,599	3.6
1975	7,639	15,373	23,012	5,237	28,249	28,249	3,820	—

Source: SG/MEC/June 1975

TABLE 10

GROWTH OF BRAZIL'S GROSS INTERNAL PRODUCT

Year	*Percent*
1967	4.8
1968	9.3
1969	9.0
1970	9.5
1971	11.3
1972	10.4
1973	11.4
1974	9.6

Source: Miniplan/IPEA/IBGE

The most notable development with regard to educational finance, as of mid-1976, concerns the *salário-educação*. In October 1975 President Geisel signed a decree-law reorganizing the *salário-educação*. Whereas in the past businesses were required to contribute to the *salário-educação* based upon the number of workers on their payroll, the new legislation requires that the formula for contributions also include members of the board of directors and company managers. Officials estimated that the new decree-law would bring about more than 1 billion cruzeiros in additional revenue.

In December 1975 the President signed a decree regulating the October 1975 law. It set a new quota (2.5 percent as opposed to the former rate of 1.4 percent) that firms must pay *before* tax exemptions are calculated. Also, states were free to levy their own *salário-educação* (0.6 percent).

Of the total amount collected, the federal government would disburse two-thirds to states, territories, and the Federal District, and one-third to the National Fund for Educational Development.

4
First-Level Education

BRAZILIAN children between seven and fourteen are entitled to eight years of free and compulsory first-level schooling. The four years of compulsory and free education decreed by successive Brazilian Constitutions were doubled by Law no. 5,692 of 1971 which, furthermore, enriched the curricula of grades five through eight with compulsory vocational training courses.

ORGANIZATION

The changes stipulated in Law no. 5,692, Brazil's Basic Education Reform Law, can be more easily understood against the background of the Law of Bases and Directives of 1961 and the organization of education it established.

Until 1971, Brazilian education consisted of three levels: primary (four years), middle-level (first-cycle or *ginásio*, four years; and second-cycle or *colégio*, three or four years), and higher. Middle-level school in both its cycles consisted of three branches: secondary, technical, and normal school (for primary-school teachers' training). Technical school again offered three options: industrial, agricultural, and commercial. All three branches of middle-level education were equivalent in qualifying a student for admission to higher education. In reality, however, the secondary, or purely academic, branch was considered the most prestigious and attracted more than 80 percent of all *ginásio* students.

The new first-level school created by the 1971 Law thus combines the former primary school and the *ginásio* (see table 11); it establishes a *núcleo comun* (core curriculum) of general studies for the eight years, and includes practical courses for all, called 'special studies,' in grades five through eight, to 'determine vocational aptitudes.' The *núcleo comun* consists of (1) Communication and Expressions—Portuguese; (2) Social Studies—history, geography, and Brazilian social and political organization, and (3) Sciences—mathematics, physics and biology. In grades five and six the student familiarizes himself with the four vocational areas or *técnicas*—industrial, commercial, agricultural, and home education. He may then chose the one most suitable for him and concentrate on it for the last two years.

By complementing general academic studies with compulsory practical courses, the new curriculum in grades five through eight serves both the so far irreconcilable goals of Brazilian basic education: to prepare youngsters for further schooling while also preparing them for the world of work. Any student willing and able to continue his studies can, as before, go on to second-level school and, ultimately, to a university; on the other hand, the masses of youngsters for whom the eighth grade will mean the end of school will be prepared to enter the labor market with only a minimum of additional vocational training. Basic schooling thus becomes 'terminal' as well as 'transitional.'

While the Reform Law tries to make the transition from study to work as smooth as possible, it also pares down the pedagogic obstacles blocking student progression in school. As its most important academic innovation, the Law completely reverses the archaically rigid norms for evaluating students' performances. Traditionally, Brazilian education was selective at all its levels; progression from primary school to *ginásio* and from there to *colégio* was controlled, and in essence blocked off for the majority of the candidates, by stiff admission exams. In fact, that selectivity started already in primary school which was from the outset geared to 'graduating' a certain small proportion of its students and not at all to providing a minimum education for all. A student's

TABLE 11

THE STRUCTURE OF BRAZILIAN PRIMARY AND MIDDLE-LEVEL/ FIRST-LEVEL AND SECOND-LEVEL EDUCATION

Former System			Present System	Ag
		Apprentice Training		18
MIDDLE-LEVEL EDUCATION	*COLÉGIO* (Second-Cycle)	SECONDARY Classical Scientific Other TECHNICAL Industrial Agricultural Commercial Other TEACHER TRAINING	SECOND-LEVEL SCHOOLING	17 1 1
	GINÁSIO (First-Cycle)	SECONDARY COMMERCIAL INDUSTRIAL AGRICULTURAL TEACHER TRAINING	FIRST-LEVEL SCHOOLING	1 1 1 1
PRIMARY EDUCATION				

Source: MEC

promotion, or failure, at the end of each year had always been determined, exclusively, by the results obtained in his year-end exams, with total disregard of whatever else he might have achieved in class. In sharp contrast, the Law here prescribes 'qualitative' rating to prevail over 'quantitative,' and that 'the results obtained during the school year shall *predominate* over those obtained in the final exam' (emphasis added).

While these innovations are revolutionary in scope, they have in the eyes of many Brazilian educators so far merely compounded the traditional quandaries of Brazil's basic education. Plagued by a combination of inherent pedagogic and extraneous socioeconomic problems, Brazil's education system had never been able to make even four years of basic schooling truly 'universal.' How could this same system suddenly be expected to provide eight years of classes for all of Brazil's schoolage children? And, further, how could it complement the relatively inexpensive academic instruction with practical classes requiring special facilities, special materials and, most important, specially trained instructors?

ENROLLMENTS

Since 1964, the public sector has significantly increased its share in what is now called grades five through eight of basic education. The former primary school which was 88 percent public in 1964 was 90 percent public in 1973. But whereas only 44.5 percent of the former *ginásio* (first-cycle middle-level school) were public in 1964, they were 70 percent public by 1973.

In overall terms, the growth of first-level schooling has been impressive. Enrollments doubled between 1965 and 1975, rising from 11,586,503 to 23,258,600. But these splendid statistics conceal a problem which becomes visible when one analyzes them by age groups: in 1975, the number of children between seven and fourteen, for whom first-level school was legally compulsory, was estimated at 22,169,195. Of those, only 18,883,227 were in school. Thus, even though the available first-level school places *exceeded* the theoretically required total by nearly one million, they remained inadequate.

The problem is analyzed in detail in a study published by the MEC in 1974. The study notes that, in 1973, the number of children between seven and fourteen enrolled in grades one through eight was 16,425,455, out of a total enrollment of 19,486,947 students which included 2,025,705 youngsters between fifteen and nineteen. Upon analyzing the distribution of enrollments throughout the eight grades, it was further found that 3,127,410 students between twelve and fourteen were still in the first four grades. The presence of this student contingent in that level of education, as well as that of students between sixteen and nineteen in the last four grades, was mainly the result of the high rates of children forced to repeat a year, and of those entering first grade at eight, nine, or ten years of age, showing a high rate of 'overmatriculation' in first-level schools.

Overmatriculation, however, is offset by dropout rates. The progressive attrition of Brazil's school population is usually illustrated with 'educational pyramids.' Such a pyramid has as its base an initial cohort of 1,000 children entering first grade of first-level school in a given year, and shows their progression through eleven consecutive years up to graduation from second-level school. What is shown mainly is, of course, a grievous thinning out of student numbers from broad base to dwindling top, whence the designation 'pyramid.'

For example, of 1,000 children entering first grade in 1952, only thirty made it into the final year of second-level school (at the time still called *colégio*) in 1962, and of those only thirteen were admitted to higher education in 1963. All of the others either had to repeat a year (or several), or else dropped out of school altogether, the bulk of them right after first grade.

Government officials usually point towards the respectable broadening at the top of the pyramid in recent years: between 1963 and 1973, the ratio of university admissions (out of first-grade entrants eleven years ago) expanded from thirteen to sixty-three

TABLE 12

BRAZIL'S EDUCATIONAL PYRAMID

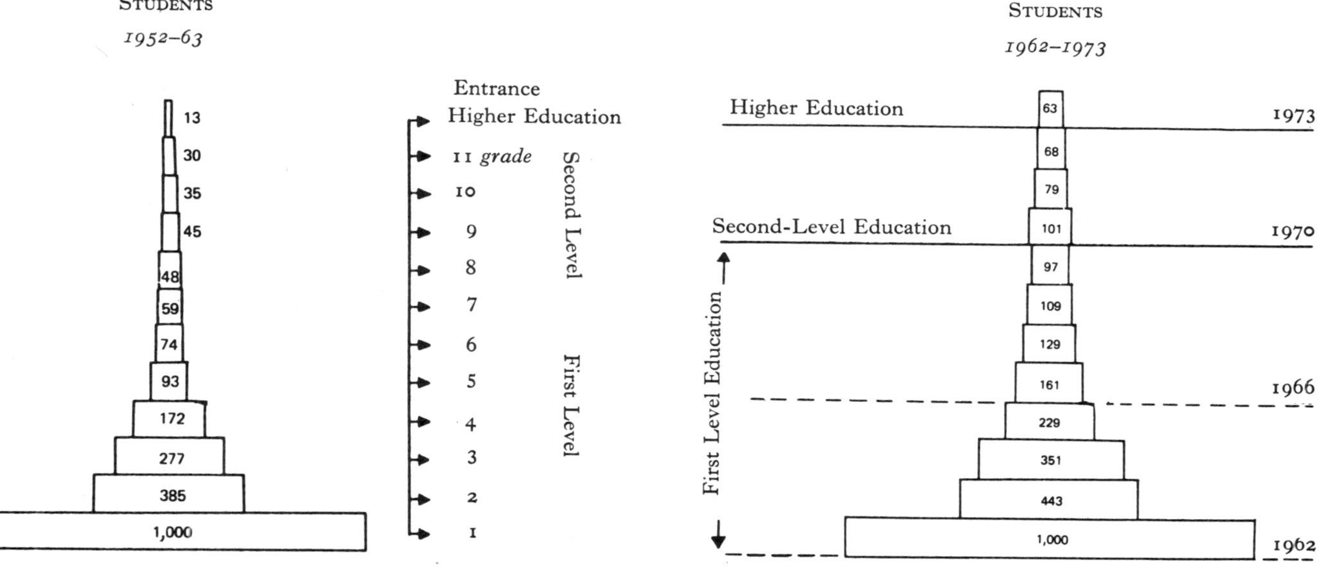

Source: SEEC/MEC as presented by Education Minister Jarbas Passarinho at '*Encontro dos Dirigentes*,' Brasília, January 1974.

(see table 12). Educators, on the other hand, point to the insufficient rates of improvement in the lower grades: while at the end of 1955 only 172 of the original 1,000 children managed to finish fourth grade, that proportion had still not risen above 229 by 1965.

Even today only one-fourth of the children in first-level schools can expect to complete the eight grades. The others will drop out somewhere along the road. Not surprisingly, the rate of attrition remains critical mainly in rural areas and in Brazil's vast and sparsely settled hinterlands with their continually migrant populations of rural workers' families. Schools, so far as they exist at all, are widely scattered. Children often must walk for miles to get there and as a rule attend classes only when they are not needed to help with the work at home. Most of Brazil's rural schools are one-room schools and often do not go beyond first grade (see table 13).

As to urban and rural enrollment rates, figures from the 1970 Census show that of 19,326,100 children between seven and fourteen years of age, 10,057,300 (52 percent) lived in urban areas, and 9,268,800 (48 percent) in rural areas. Enrollments totalled 13,190,315, with twice as many children from urban areas (8,848,571) as from rural regions (4,341,744). Thus, while the enrollment rate of the age-group was 68.25 percent nationwide, the rate was only 46.84 percent for children in rural areas, as against 87.98 percent for children in the cities (see table 14).

TEACHING BODY

Teacher qualification, too, varies greatly. Little more than 50 percent of the teachers in grades one to four, the former primary school, have completed normal second-level school and are thus fully qualified. For grades five to eight, the former *ginásio*, less than 30 percent of the teachers have the required four years higher education which include a year's pedagogic studies. Second-level normal schools, nearly exclusively attended by girls, are concentrated in the developed southern states of Rio de Janeiro, São

TABLE 13

FIRST-LEVEL EDUCATION—DISTRIBUTION OF ENROLLMENTS—1971–73

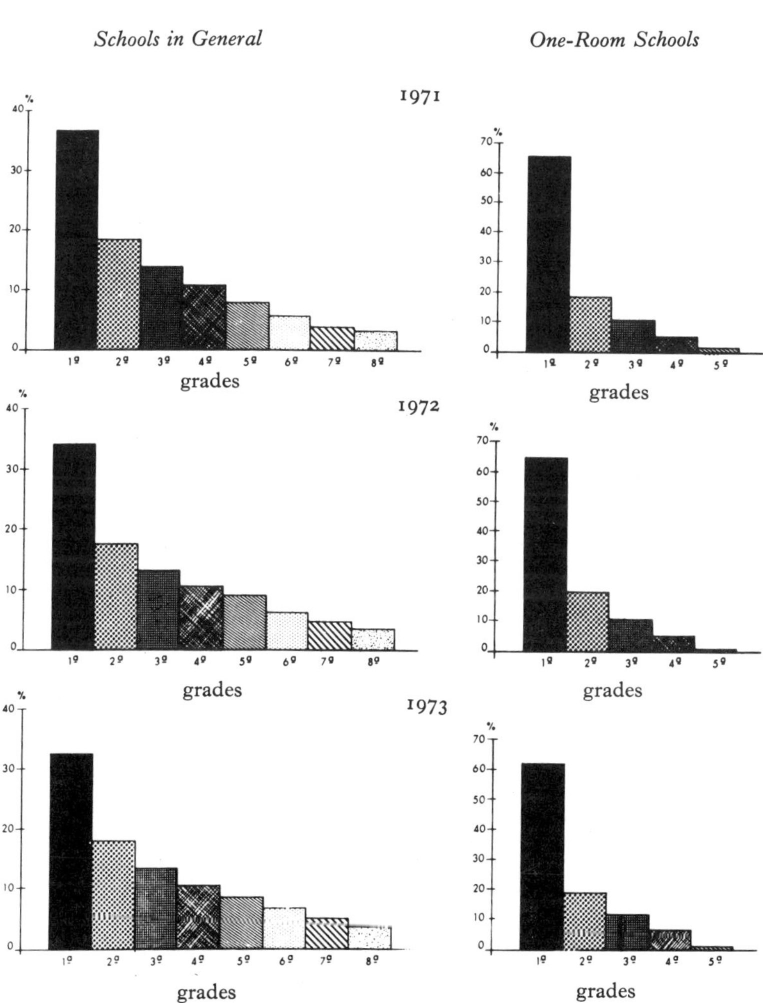

Source: *Estatísticas da Educação Nacional,* 1971–73 SEEC/MEC p. 83

TABLE 14

ENROLLMENT RATES ACCORDING TO LOCATION—1970

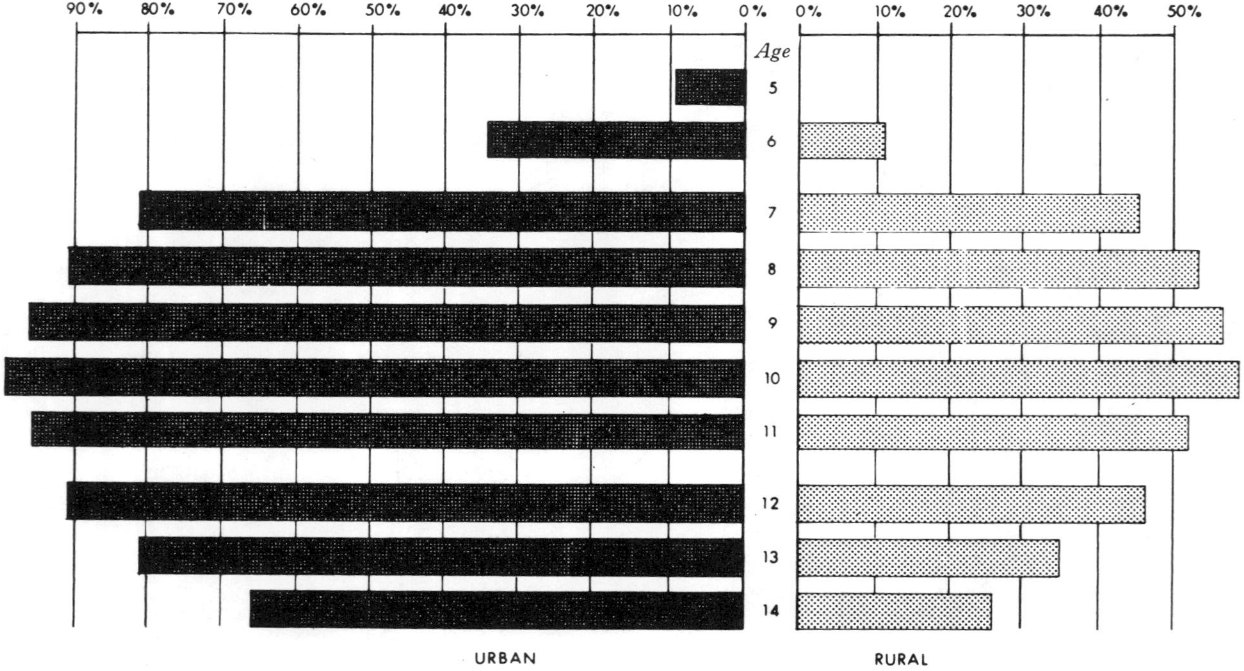

Source: *Estatísticas da Educação Nacional* 1960–71 SEEC/MEC p. 17

Paulo, Minas Gerais, Paraná, and Rio Grande do Sul. While 100 percent of the primary teachers in the cities of Rio de Janeiro and São Paulo are credentialled, in Brazil's rural areas nonqualified teachers, half of whom have themselves only primary education or even less, predominate.

Nonqualified teachers as a rule appear to have no idea of what happens in the heads of their pupils or how to motivate them to learn. Being essentially untrained and often unsure themselves, these teachers usually insist on scholastic 'standards' with unrelenting rigidity. Right from the start they tend to focus their efforts only on their most promising pupils, usually no more than half of the group in any class, and leave the others aside. For example, a first grade child in a Brazilian rural school who is not literate after three or four months will find himself or herself academically shunted aside.

Yet without these nonqualified teachers there would often be no rural schools at all. Long treks to and from school, on muleback, or in canoes, are still the accepted modes of travelling for teachers as well as their pupils in some of Brazil's pockets of poverty in the Northeast and the North, and even in some areas of Rio Grande do Sul. The low salaries paid by the municipalities, often far below regional minimum salaries, act as a further spur for all who can make it possible to upgrade their qualifications in summer vacation retraining courses, in order to try to find work in urban areas instead.

IMPLEMENTING BASIC EDUCATION POLICIES

There is thus a great deal of realism in the Reform Law's stipulation that it should be implemented gradually and flexibly to suit the conditions and possibilities of each state. The MEC's immediate goal is, admittedly, to achieve eight years' schooling in the urban areas of the large municipalities, and to strive for four years in rural townships and periferal areas. The Law foresees that during an unspecified transition period schools which do not yet have the full eight years may start vocational courses in the lower grades. Modernized curricula and the abolishment of rigid and unrealistic standards for year-end promotion, as prescribed in the Law, should further ease the children's road.

However, it is today increasingly admitted that the crux of the problem may be less structural and pedagogic than socioeconomic. State governments have made their own surveys to look for the roots of their educational problems. Whereas failure and dropout rates formerly were attributed to a failure of the schools, they are today recognized as being chiefly the consequence of social problems. A study prepared in Minas Gerais found that one of the main causes for its schools' 'lack of retention' (the sum of failures and dropouts) was poverty, pure and simple, with all its consequences: nutritional, sanitary, and cultural deficiencies, compounded by the children's need to work in their earliest years.

In Bahia, one of Brazil's northeastern states, an education survey for 1973 showed that only 6 percent of first-level school students continued into eighth grade and that the chief culprit was hunger, responsible for half the dropouts in each grade. The decline in dropout rates in Salvador, Bahia's capital, from 84 percent in 1970 to 48 percent in 1975, was attributed solely to a stepped up distribution of school lunches which, admittedly, constitute one of the chief attractions for schoolage children in Brazil's poor areas. The expansion of Brazil's National School Lunch Program (CNAE) suffered a temporary setback in 1973 when it lost its financial support from international agencies because of the famines in Africa and Asia. But CNAE now has ample funding from the National Educational Development Fund (FNDE). In 1975, 11.5 million Brazilian first-level school children in 3,500 townships received school lunches, and by 1979 all children should receive them.

Social programs—health, sanitation, nutrition, education—to bridge the gulf between Brazil's rich and poor people are given priority rating and funds in Brazil's Second National Development

Plan, 1975–1979. The first plan (1971–1974) allocated US$ 10 billion, from public and private sources, to education in all its phases. But educators and progressive politicians have for years rebuked the federal government for its failure, as they see it, to expand its *budgetary* allocations to basic education which affects the largest share of the school population. For years the argument has been waged around the regularly *in*creasing sums but *de*creasing proportions of the federal budget allocated to education as a whole, as well as the fact that the MEC has for years allocated more than half of its funds to higher education.

The fact that the MEC's budget represents little more than one-fourth of the monies, both public and private, spent on Brazilian education has done little to subdue the argument. Equally controversial, in the eyes of some, is the federal government's endeavor to increase education funding from extra-budgetary sources. In May 1976 a group of Senators drafted a bill intended to give education a *fixed* share of 12 percent of the federal budget (and raise the shares contributable by states and municipalities to 24 percent). But right from the outset it was seen likely that the government would refuse to be bound by the outmoded rigidity of a fixed budgetary allocation, for education or any other purposes. To no one's surprise, therefore, the Senate, under strong government pressure, permitted the bill to lapse by 'failing' to provide the quorum needed to vote on it on the Senate floor.

PRESCHOOL EDUCATION

One area where lack of funds, poverty, and general societal dysfunctions become most dramatically evident is Brazil's still embryonic preschool education.

The Basic Education Reform Law mentions preschool education only in broadest terms. It says that 'the [state and municipal education] systems shall see to it that children under seven years of age receive suitable education in nursery schools, kindergartens, and similar institutions.' The Law thus establishes a general responsibility but refrains from formulating specific or normative stipulations.

Educators involved in drafting the Law claim that at the time this apparent neglect of preschool education was meant to be an unavoidable, and strictly transitory, postponement: it would have been unrealistic to reform and expand basic education while simultaneously building up Brazil's practically nonexistent preschool education.

Since 1971, Brazil's preschool education has suffered from what could be called the backlash of the generalized efforts to comply with Law 5,692 which makes education compulsory for children between seven and fourteen: state and municipal attention is focusing on that age group, exclusively. For example, in São Paulo, which as a rule is ahead of the rest of Brazil in questions of education, only 8.5 percent of the children between three and six were attending state and municipal kindergartens in 1972. That percentage had slightly *decreased* in 1974. An increase in the number of municipal kindergartens was more than offset by the decrease of those maintained by the State Education Secretariat, admittedly no longer directly interested in providing preschool education.

Also, before Law 5,692 many of the former primary schools had maintained preschool education classes. As a result of the new guidelines these schools turned their attention towards providing, gradually, grades five, six, seven, and eight of the new first-level education—*instead of* the former kindergarten classes.

On the other hand, Brazil's progressive educators have become increasingly convinced that the effectiveness of first-level schools will, undoubtedly and inevitably, continue being stymied by their students' high failure rates in the early grades, and particularly in the first grade (see table 12), unless the basic causes for these failures are recognized and tackled in the children's preschool years. In spite of the nationwide rise in promotions from first grade, resulting from the gradual implementation of Law no. 5,692, the first grade failure rate in 1976 still represented 63 percent of the total failures in grades one through four.

A few figures illustrate the magnitude of the problem of attempting to provide preschool education for Brazilian children. The 1970 Census figures show nearly 19.5 million children to six years of age, representing 20.9 percent of Brazil's population. By 1975 that number had grown to 21 million. About 15 million were children between two and six, of whom only 570,000, or 3.8 percent, enjoyed any type of preschool education. Or, if one focuses on the two years preceding first-level school enrollment, Brazil's five- and six-year olds, only 7 percent of that age-group have access to preschool education, which is predominantly private and attended mainly by children from urban middle-class families.

This potentially staggering task is heavily weighted with the deficiencies rooted in poverty and underdevelopment: hunger, inadequate health care, and cultural deprivation. Children lacking in proper nutrition and health care, an estimated 70 percent of all Brazilian children between two and six, supply the massive contingents doomed to failure in their first years of school. And their cultural deprivation, a phenomenon well known even in developed nations among children of migrant rural workers or those living in inner-city ghetto areas, today results to a large extent from Brazil's soaring urbanization rate. Between 1960 and 1970, Brazil's urban population increased by 62.7 percent, whereas its rural population grew by only 6.9 percent.

Masses of people from rural areas flood the peripheries of Brazilian cities woefully unable to provide even minimum services. Brazil's rural families as a rule can adapt to the demands and complexities of a diversified urban society only with difficulty and, at best, only partially. They survive at precarious economic levels and, together with the urban poor, they develop marginal life styles with social and cultural patterns unsuited to cope with the challenges of city life. For their children, this so-called 'culture of poverty' constitutes a practically insurmountable barrier to their assimilating education as it is offered in Brazilian schools.

Among a number of recent studies in the preschool child area, probably the most interesting one was made by Ana Maria

Poppovic at the Carlos Chagas Foundation in São Paulo. The study shows that almost half of the children who fail in first grade do so because: (1) the school system into which they are expected to integrate is not prepared to receive them, since its instruction presupposes a minimum of indispensable knowledge and ability; and (2) they come from economically deprived families and are in no way prepared for the demands of school. The study adduces Deutsch's 'hidden curriculum,' the sum of social, cultural, and learning influences to which a child is exposed from birth to school age, which are so rich in middle and upper classes and so rudimentary in homes of poorer people.

According to the study, a poor six-year-old child in São Paulo barely succeeds in equaling the performance of a rich four-year-old child. From then on, performance differences increase with age to constitute a 'cumulative deficit.' To prevent this, an 'intervention curriculum' would have to be elaborated to help the 'culturally marginalized children,' who constitute 60 percent of the children under six in the state of São Paulo. The cost of such an 'intervention curriculum' would, unquestionably, be high but also 'extremely compensatory' by signally reducing first-grade failure rates, and resulting in social gains all around.

São Paulo's first preschool 'experimental program for cultural enrichment' was started in 1972 among poor children living in the city's periphery. The program relied heavily on the cooperation of the children's mothers, as monitors and supervisors, and thus helped the mothers as well as the children. In 1973, the performance of these children who had by then entered first grade was measured against that of control group of children from the same surroundings who had not taken part in the experiment. Only 10 percent from either group achieved grades comparable to the average grades of middle-class children. But 60 percent of the experimental group performed at levels just slightly below that average, as compared to only 10 percent from the control group. Furthermore, while nearly 30 percent of the experimental group were still considered as likely to fail at the end of first grade, that proportion was more than 80 percent for the control group.

The data of the Carlos Chagas Foundation study and their implications for first-level school performance are quoted in the MEC's 1974 Preschool Education Project. The project also analyzes age-group distortion rates in first-level school, and their roots in deficient preschool education, but goes far beyond the experts' analyses of 'educational pyramids.' Fully aware that preschool education cannot be limited merely to preschool 'instruction' but must also encompass nutrition and health care, the project outlines possible remedial programs, stressing the weight of their extra-educational components. The project then suggests a number of test programs, to be implemented by the MEC together with health authorities, Social Security, the National Nutrition Institute, et al. However, before going into all its varied suggestions, the project also states quite clearly: 'Whereas first-level schooling is constitutionally compulsory, and so long as available resources are insufficient to pay for the fulfilment of this obligation, there are few possibilities for real service to the preschool child.'

Which means that the dilemma will be around for a long time. Except that while the dilemma lasts, the true iniquities of Brazil's school system must be expected to remain glaringly evident. Education may today be one of the chief factors of social and social mobility in Brazil (see table 2), but, conversely, the essentially socioeconomic selectivity of Brazilian schools still represents the greatest obstacle for poor children ever to get beyond the early grades, let alone beyond first-level school.

As is often true in Brazil where a problem can only be solved by 'the government' and no one else, at least one maverick has shown up here, too. In Curitiba, the capital of Paraná, in the south, a new preschool program is operating successfully; it is based on community groups and draws on help from state education, health, and welfare agencies. Among other things, children under six are being taught basic notions of health, hygiene, and nutrition. There are no 'homogenous curricula' because teachers are free to adapt to the peculiarities of the community groups. Children further are shown how to care for a truck-garden, and their parents are encouraged to plant fruit and vegetables to supplement their diet. In other words, wherever possible, the work with the children is complemented by guidance for parents. Curitiba maintains twenty-one municipal first-level schools and the preschool program is being given in fourteen of them.

5

Second-Level Education

BRAZIL's new second-level eduction, the former *colégio*, has so far proved to be eminently controversial, and difficult to implement. At that level, too, Law 5,692 stipulates that the academic curriculum must be complemented with work-oriented training, called 'special studies,' for all. Aside from being unpopular with much of its clientele, the compulsory work-oriented training has been found to be inconvenient, expensive, and, initially, beyond the reach of most schools.

ENROLLMENTS

In relative terms, the second-level school has expanded at twice the rate of first-level school: matriculations nearly quadrupled between 1965 and 1975, increasing from 509,110 to 1,937,023. The total rate of dropouts up to graduation remained fairly steady at less than 40 percent. The MEC plans to increase the number of second-level school enrollments to 2.5 million by 1979.

ORGANIZATION BEFORE 1971

Up to 1971, the diversity of *colégio* education in its different branches—secondary (i.e., purely academic), normal, commercial, technical-industrial, and agricultural—could have represented a great diversity of professional options for its graduates, but in reality turned out to be nothing of the kind (see table 15). About

TABLE 15

MIDDLE-LEVEL EDUCATION

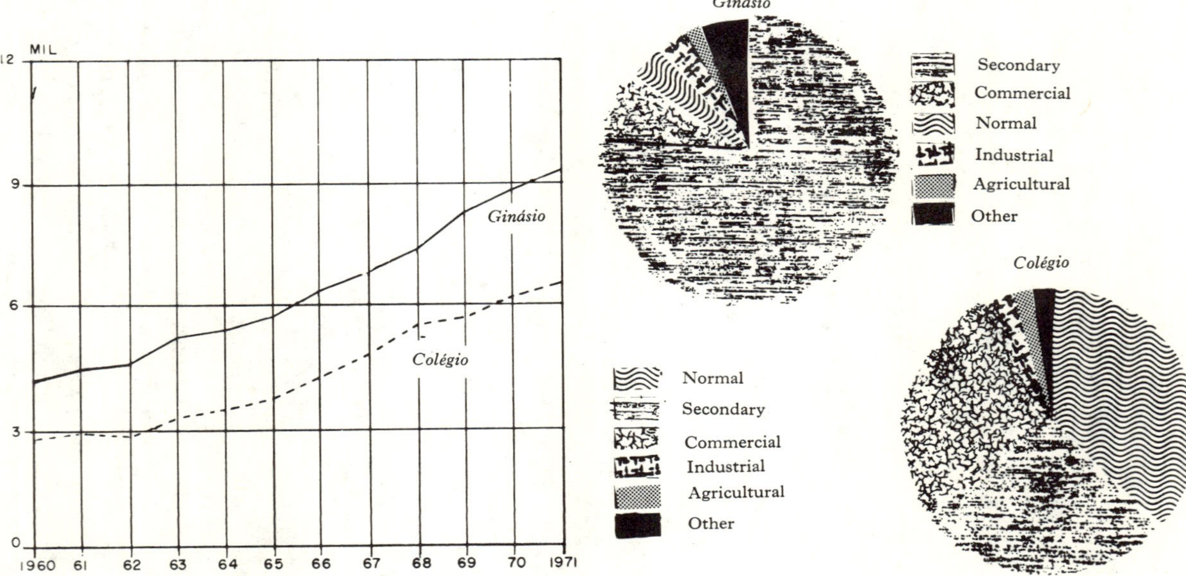

Source: *Estatísticas da Educação Nacional 1960–71* SEEC/MEC p. 63

90 percent of *all colégio graduates* traditionally aimed at university admission.

To begin with, the overwhelming majority of *colégios* was academic to cater to their clients' demands for university preparatory education; their curricula were predominantly either humanistic or scientific, but in fact were always geared towards the great areas of university admission examinations, the *vestibulares*. Normal *colégios*, which were supposed to provide the urgently needed primary-school teachers, proved for more than half of their graduates to have been merely a stretch of the road towards higher education. Commercial *colégios* were in demand mainly by less qualified students who could cope with their less stringent academic standards and still be entitled to compete for access to higher education. Industrial and technical education at the *colégio* level was given by a few public technical schools, whose usually excellent professional curricula were sparsely bolstered with academic courses. The same was the case at the handful of agricultural *colégios*. Graduates from both these branches, too, dreamed of higher education whenever possible.

The effect of this diversified *colégio* education thus worked out to be catastrophic from two points of view: (1) candidates with widely divergent, and usually inadequate, academic qualifications battered at the doors of Brazilian universities which as a rule were hard pressed to admit even half their number; of those, only about 15 percent went on to graduation; and (2) all the others remained in limbo somewhere along the road—ill-prepared or, in the case of secondary *colégio* graduates, totally unprepared for Brazilian labor markets.

THE NEW SECOND-LEVEL EDUCATION

The new second-level school was thus projected to remedy both these shortcomings. Its *núcleo comun* of general studies was geared to assist those for whom second-level education would, as before, remain 'transitory' on their way to higher education; its 'professionalizing' courses for all were meant to serve those—in growing numbers, it was hoped—for whom second-level school would be 'terminal' and who would thus be able to find jobs as well-prepared 'middle-level' professionals.

This, at least, was the idea of the reform. In practice, it has so far worked out to be one part law and three parts loopholes.

The least controversial of the innovations—although there have been quibbles about that, too—has been the *núcleo comun* of general studies now stipulated for all second-level schools. Whereas in first-level schools subject matters are taught in integrated 'areas,' they are taught in second-level school in individual disciplines: Portuguese, Brazilian literature, history, geography, mathematics, physical and biological sciences, civic studies, one foreign language (usually English, or else English and French), plus sports, introduction to arts, and health education.

'PROFESSIONALIZING' EDUCATION CYCLE

Depending on what type of professionalization one aims for (tertiary, secondary, or primary) total hours of instruction can vary between 2,200 and 2,900, and must include 300 to 1,200 hours of professional training (the latter in a four-year course). The number of class hours for each of the general disciplines may be adjusted to a proportion most suitable for the student's professional goal.

The uproar was caused, not all that surprisingly, by the new compulsory 'professionalization.' The Law suggested the creation of 'interschool centers' to serve the different second-level schools for their professionalizing courses. Or else, the schools should try to work together with enterprises to provide the students' practical training. The specifics of the professionalizing courses were left up to the State Education Councils and were to be based on local labor market demands.

But even though it was of course left up to each school, or each group of schools, to choose which, and how many, of the professions to teach, most of them used the admittedly complex and inconvenient specificity of training required as a pretext to resort to subterfuge, if not outright noncompliance.

In first-level school, 'vocational aptitude testing' and 'work initiation' are channeled into four chief 'areas': industrial, commercial, agricultural, and home education. In second-level school, the Law's stipulation of 'professional certification' was initially interpreted to mean, exclusively, complete training for an individual, specific profession. And there are about 130 different 'middle-level' professions in Brazil.

What is perhaps most remarkable is that some few schools—in regions as far apart as Pernambuco, Rio de Janeiro State, and Rio Grande do Sul—succeeded in implementing rapidly both the letter and the spirit of the reform and in coping with its initial complexity.

For example, an 'educational complex' thirty miles north of Rio de Janeiro organized itself in early 1972 by linking three formerly independent schools. They pooled facilities, students, professors, and resources. Equipment and machinery was financed with bank loans and the 'complex' administered like a business enterprise. In early 1973, the complex offered its students thirty-one professional certifications. The different curricula were compiled with an academic credit system. The thirty-one professions were divided into four training 'groups': commerce and services; social-pedagogic training; health and biology; and technology. The rationale for that was that some professions, such as civil construction, and hydraulic or electric installation, had a number of different technical courses in common, and that, to give another example, commercial and business techniques would have to be learned by students in administrative courses as well as by those training to work in real-estate.

Basing its decision in part on the experiences gained in these few schools, the CFE offered an alternative to 'professional education' in the form of 'professionalizing' education, in a ruling of January 1975. It introduced the concept of 'basic certification' which places greater stress than before on general education, and reduces the weight of specific technical education. Students should acquire enough technological knowledge to be able to adapt to various occupations; specific training could be completed on the job. The 'professionalizing' part of the curriculum would consist of courses linked to an ample number of professional competencies, in a determined area. The student would thus get 'basic certification,' or education for work, and graduate from second-level school with the option of entering the labor market, or else going on to higher education; or, if he wanted 'specific competency,' to continue for a fourth year of second-level school to get his diploma of 'middle-level professional,' or *técnico*.

What is being aimed at, according to a member of the MEC, is the German *Berufsaufbauschule* (but which would, in Brazil, supersede and eliminate the *Gymnasium*, if one wants to continue the comparison with the German model).

THE DOMINANCE OF PRIVATE SCHOOLS

The problem, even with the more flexible 'professionalizing' education, is due largely to the structure of Brazilian second-level education which was always exclusively urban, and remained predominantly private up to 1964. Between 1964 and 1972, the share of private second-level education decreased from 58 percent to 42 percent. It is these private schools, both Catholic and secular, and by tradition predominantly academic, which have put up the stiffest resistance to professionalizing education.

Private schools usually taught the full eight grades of the former middle-level education (*ginásio* and *colégio*) (see table 11) and, Catholic schools (traditionally called *colégios*, whatever the level of their studies), often taught the full range from kindergarten to second-level school graduation. Private schools have been hardest hit at the former *ginásio* level, where their participation shrank from 55.5 percent in 1964 to 31.5 percent in 1972. With the reform, which makes the former *ginásio* an integral, compulsory, and tuition-free part of first-level school, the private schoools' calamitous situation worsened and was relieved only, to an insufficient extent, by a scant number of scholarships bought by State Education Secretariats for needy students for whom no places could be found in public schools.

In 1975, about half of the 1.5 million places available in Brazilian private schools remained unfilled, partly because of the growing competition by public schools. One educator explained the obvious: when parents of limited means are faced with the choice between keeping their child in a fairly good, but paid, private school and in a passable, but tuition-free, public school, they always opt for the latter. Thus, only the best private schools survive.

Here again, even the survivors are divided in their reactions, depending on their locations. A number of Catholic *colégios* in the periphery of Rio de Janeiro, for example, have effortlessly 'grouped' themselves, sharing facilities, students, and professors. Each unit specializes in a specific area (humanities, sciences, etc.) for all, and professionalizing courses are given at an 'interschool center.' Schools and students, whatever the latter's ultimate goals, have adjusted to the reform. The system of grouping, at least for professionalizing courses, has also been adopted successfully by Rio's best Catholic *colégios*, which cater to the children of Rio's wealthiest families, but here the opposition to the reform continues to be vehement. They resent the 'imposition' of professionalizing education for which, they claim, they cannot motivate their students who are culled from a socially and economically privileged class and aim, exclusively, infallibly and, on the whole, successfully for a university education.

Public second-level schools, with a clientele far more oriented towards the labor market, so far usually lack the means to offer professionalizing education in an efficient manner. This, at least, is the general picture as painted in gloomiest terms whenever public and private school administrators meet for their periodic regional gatherings. It is more convenient, cheaper and easier all around to continue as before. And, anyway, 99 percent of all second-level school students, now as before, aim towards higher education.

IMPLEMENTING SECOND-LEVEL EDUCATION POLICIES

The reform has thus been implemented spottily. Goiás, a not overly developed state in the Center-West out of whose heart the Federal District, Brasília, was carved, started in early 1973 to create twenty-three 'intercomplementary centers' to provide professionalizing courses to all its public second-level schools. In sharp contrast, São Paulo had 721 public second-level schools (concentrated in 295 of the State's 571 municipalities) of which, in 1973, 668 had neither facilities nor machinery to give professionalizing courses. By 1974, about a fourth of the total were labelled as being 'professionalizing' but, in fact, consisted mainly of the old commercial and normal schools. The creation of new—and, admittedly, expensive—interschool centers, on the basis of regional labor market surveys, was only ponderously getting beyond the planning stage. However, most of São Paulo's private *colégios* had by then in theory implemented the reform. They showed a certain number of professionalizing courses on their program for legal purposes, but continued to give academic instruction in those so-called 'technical' classes. The *colégio* directors claimed that students and parents favored the subterfuge because technical instruction was of no value for university admission.

The identical attitude was professed by the director of a great private *colégio* in Rio who admitted openly, in October 1975, that his school was using various shortcuts to comply, in theory, with the dictates of the Law without, in fact, changing anything in his courses. Their names were changed: chemistry was transformed into 'fundamentals of laboratory techniques,' mathematics became 'applied calculus.' And the students continued doing in their classes what they always did: preparing themselves for the *vestibulares*. Only the appearance of professionalization was kept up.

The MEC had, of course, recognized as early as 1973 that only strong motivation of some kind would get second-level schools, both public and private, to implement the reform with some speed. The means hit upon by the CFE was to grant additional points in the *vestibulares* to students who could give proof that they had absolved professionalizing courses, even though they aimed for university admission. The thought behind the CFE's decision, translated into a formal decree, to take effect nationwide as of 1975, was that it would make the students and their families put some pressure on the laggard second-level schools to secure these obvious advantages for their clientele by finally providing the controversial professionalizing courses.

The effect of the ruling, however, was exactly the opposite of what had been intended. Educators protested the ruling as unfair and 'discriminatory,' since it would give undue advantages to the few who had been fortunate enough to graduate from schools which had already implemented the reform. Students and their families gleefully joined in the fray. Under this multifaceted pressure the effective date of the decree had to be postponed, to 1977, and a further postponement, probably *sine die*, is more than likely, and thus also the eventual demise of the well-intended decree altogether.

On the other hand, of course, precisely the fact that professionalization does *not* count towards university admission slows down the reform's implementation.

6

Higher Education

BRAZIL lacked an organized system of higher education as well as a true university up until the second decade of the twentieth century. Since then, however, an initially slow expansion turned into a virtual runaway growth up to 1973, when the growth rate again slowly began to taper off.

STRUCTURE, ADMINISTRATION, AND FINANCE

Brazil today has fifty-seven universities, thirty-seven of which are federal, state, or municipal institutions and charge only nominal tuition fees. Nine of the private universities are secular; the others are affiliated with the Roman Catholic Church of Brazil. There are, further, 5 college federations and 786 isolated, single-purpose colleges (*faculdades isoladas*—a higher education institution which is unaffiliated with a university or consortium of colleges, e.g., a School of Design) of which 77 percent are private.

Regionally, 86.1 percent of all postsecondary institutions are located in Brazil's most developed part, the southern and southeastern states.

To be a university, an educational institution must comprise five or more institutes, must have been operating for at least three years, and must receive recognition from the Federal Education Council. The chief normative structure is the Council of Rectors of Brazilian Universities, a voluntary association of university rectors who meet at frequent intervals to debate all aspects of higher education.

A University Council (senate) functions as a policymaking body within the university. It consists of the deans and full professors of the various schools as well as delegates, representing associate and assistant professors, and students. In the past, a *professor catedrático* (roughly translated as a professor holding an endowed chair) controlled each discipline within the school. In recent years, Brazil has moved to a system of professorial rank—assistant, associate, and full professor—in which tenure may be granted, but the power and autonomy is far less than that of the *cátedra* (chair). In addition, in compliance with the 1968 University Reform Law (No. 5,540), colleges and universities are moving towards a system of 'departmentalization.'

At the undergraduate level, courses of study vary from three to six years; and, in contrast with the U.S. system of higher education, the curriculum includes a number of courses of study which North American universities offer exclusively on the graduate level. For example, medicine is a six-year undergraduate program; law and engineering are five-year programs; and journalism, library science, and physical education are three years in length.

The cornerstone of the government's higher education policies is the 1968 University Reform Law. Among its modernizing features are provisions to break up the *faculdades* (semiautonomous colleges within the university), to introduce innovations in the curriculum, to switch to the credit system for evaluating students, and to appropriate sufficient public funds to support the expansion and improvement in the physical and human resources of higher education (e.g., more and better full-time professors).

The federal government is the source of almost all financing of federal higher education, as state governments are for state universities and colleges. Federal funds are also disbursed in lesser amounts to state and private institutions, usually for aid to poor students. The private institutions are financed, chiefly, through tuition fees, and philanthropic contributions from foundations and religious organizations.

The varied percentage growth in the MEC expenditures for higher education has been uneven due partially because of the rapid growth of enrollments and expenditures among the private institutions since 1970 (see table 16).

TABLE 16

BUDGET OF THE MINISTRY OF EDUCATION AND CULTURE, 1970–1975: ALLOCATION OF FUNDS FOR HIGHER EDUCATION
(*in January 1975 CR$ 1,000*)

	Resources				
	Total		*Higher Education*		
Year	*From the Treasury and Other Sources*	*Other Sources Only*	*Allocation*	*Percent Growth*	*Percent of Total Budget*
1970	3,309.2	134.2	2,043.9	—	61.8
1971	3,744.7	201.0	2,205.8	7.9	58.9
1972	4,307.7	826.5	2,496.9	13.2	58.0
1973	4,938.2	852.9	2,699.5	8.1	54.7
1974	5,882.1	968.5	2,862.5	6.0	49.1
1975	7,444.5	1,889.5	3,070.0	7.3	41.3

Source: General Secretariat, MEC, June 1975

Table 17 shows the national growth figures of higher education since 1969 by student body, available freshman places, and number of graduates.

Public higher education has not grown nearly as rapidly as the private colleges and universities. By 1970 private higher education enrollments started exceeding enrollments in the public sector, 50.5 to 49.5 percent (see table 18). The expansion of private colleges and universities steadily increased so that by 1974 slightly more than 63 percent of all students attended private institutions.

TABLE 17

HIGHER EDUCATION IN BRAZIL: NATIONAL TRENDS

Year	*Available freshman places yearly*	*Total Enrollment*	*Graduates*
1940	9,200	27,671	6,504
1950	14,600	48,999	8,303
1960	39,781	93,202	16,893
1961	43,240	98,892	18,226
1962	47,000	107,299	19,472
1963	51,751	124,214	18,926
1964	57,990	142,386	20,282
1965	57,469	155,781	20,793
1966	60,137	180,109	24,301
1967	80,915	212,882	30,108
1968	88,588	278,295	35,946
1969	143,008*	342,886	44,709
1970	185,277*	425,478	64,049
1971	221,645*	561,397	73,453
1972	280,209*	688,382	97,637*
1973*	320,476	811,237	129,122
1974*	348,749	897,200	150,178
1975**	365,000	940,000	163,000

Source: Ministério da Educação e Cultura, *Catálogo Geral das Instituições de Ensino Superior* (Brasília: MEC, 1974), p. 13.
* primary source data (with reference to the second semester)
** projected figures

TABLE 18

ENROLLMENTS IN HIGHER EDUCATION INSTITUTIONS BY TYPE OF CONTROL: 1970–1974

Year	*Enrollment*	*Percent in public Institutions*	*Percent in Private Institutions*
1970	425,478	49.50	50.50
1971	561,397	44.93	55.07
1972	688,382	40.44	59.56
1973	811,237	38.83	61.17
1974	897,200	36.99	63.01

Source: SEEC/MEC

During the same period, single-purpose colleges, which accounted for 47.57 percent of higher education enrollments in 1970, increased their hold to over half the postsecondary student body the following year. Enrollments in these colleges have grown steadily, and by 1974 accounted for 57.39 of the students in higher education.

While many private single-purpose colleges may, in fact, be little more than academic cesspools, it is an undeniable fact that they have taken some of the pressure off public universities and provided postsecondary schooling opportunities for students who could not secure admissions elsewhere.

ENROLLMENTS

Total enrollments in postsecondary education in Brazil are illustrated in table 19. The absolute number of matriculations as well as the growth rate are, indeed, impressive. Since 1964 undergraduate student enrollment has risen from 143,386 to 942,055 in 1975. This represents a percentage increase of 561.6 percent and an average annual rate of increase of almost 19 percent.

As to enrollments in major courses of study, table 20 shows the distribution of undergraduate enrollments by professional courses of study from 1964 to 1974. (Curiously, philosophy, sciences, and letters are classified as professions).

TABLE 19

ENROLLMENTS IN HIGHER EDUCATION BEGINNING OF ACADEMIC YEAR AND ANNUAL GROWTH RATE: 1964–1975

Year	*Enrollment*	*Growth from 1964 (Percent)*	*Annual Growth Rate (Percent)*
1964	143,386	—	—
1965	155,781	9.4	9.4
1966	180,109	26.5	15.6
1967	212,882	49.5	18.2
1968	278,295	95.4	30.7
1969	342,886	140.8	23.2
1970	425,478	198.8	24.1
1971	561,397	294.3	31.9
1972	688,382	383.5	22.6
1973	811,237	469.7	17.8
1974	897,200	530.1	10.6
1975	942,055	561.6	4.8

Source: SEEC/MEC

TABLE 20

HIGHER EDUCATION ENROLLMENT BEGINNING OF ACADEMIC YEAR: PROFESSIONAL CYLE STUDIES: 1964–1974

Year	PROGRAM									
	Business, Economics		*Medicine*		*Engineering*		*Law*		*Philosophy, Sciences, Letters, Education*	
	(Number)	*(Percent)*	*(Number)*	*(Percent)*	*(Number)*	*(Percent)*	*(Number)*	*(Percent)*	*(Number)*	*(Percent)*
1964	16,918	14.7	14,183	12.3	20,701	18.0	30,974	26.9	32,396	28.1
1965	19,751	15.5	15,574	12.4	21,986	17.3	33,608	26.4	36,314	28.5
1966	24,027	16.1	17,152	11.5	26,603	17.9	36,363	24.4	44,802	30.1
1967	28,463	16.5	20,448	11.9	28,839	16.7	41,800	24.2	52,802	30.6
1968	36,796	16.0	25,226	11.0	37,552	16.4	52,856	23.0	76,799	33.5
1969	30,642	12.5	27,726	11.3	26,015	10.6	60,525	24.6	100,984	41.0
1970	40,453	13.4	32,287	10.7	33,783	11.2	71,236	23.6	123,384	41.0
1971	52,218	14.7	30,990	8.7	39,433	11.1	76,906	21.6	156,187	43.9
1972	61,793	15.2	34,758	8.6	47,625	11.8	78,340	19.3	182,446	45.0
1973	75,991	17.6	35,357	8.2	51,851	12.0	79,621	18.5	188,441	43.7
1974	85,212	18.4	39,815	8.6	59,615	12.9	81,564	17.6	196,707	42.5

Source: SEEC/DAU/MEC

Three major trends can be noted: (1) business administration and economics have replaced law as the most popular courses of study in a society where the dominant role of technocrats is ever increasing (the former courses grew by 403.7 percent over a ten-year period as compared with 163.3 percent for law); (2) noticeably large enrollment increases have occurred in fields where instructional costs are low (e.g., philosophy, general science, and letters); and (3) enrollment declines in certain professional fields of study (i.e., medicine, engineering) are attributed not to waning student interest but calculated decisions on the part of the Federal Education Council not to authorize an increase in the number of existing schools.

ACCESS TO HIGHER EDUCATION

Admission to higher education in Brazil is determined exclusively by the candidate's performance in the college entrance examinations (*exame vestibular*).

The *exame vestibular* was created in 1911, as a state test to screen candidates for secondary school graduation diplomas. With the uncontrolled expansion of the secondary school system during the following decades, accompanied by the lowering of standards in many schools, the *vestibulares* eventually acquired the function of university entrance examinations. The seminal Law of Directives and Bases of 1961 made the *exame vestibular* compulsory for access to the university, and restated the autonomous right of higher education institutions to set up competitive exams for college admission. But, since the number of applicants consistently exceeded the number of available freshman places, the *vestibulares* turned into a numbers game to limit the number of admissions to that of available openings, instead of a process of selection for students qualified for admission. The content of examinations (often far above secondary school graduation level) and the grading system were manipulated to suit this objective.

Consequently, candidates had to rely quite heavily upon *cursos prévestibulares*. The *cursinhos*, as they are commonly called, are not a part of the formal educational system. They are privately owned and operated training courses whose sole purpose is to prepare college applicants to pass the competitive college entrance examinations. The teaching staff of *cursinhos* consists of part-time instructors. They are well-remunerated; and since they are frequently evaluated by the students, they are equally concerned about content and teaching methods.

The *cursinhos* are highly lucrative operations. They commonly engage in cutthroat competition with one another to recruit students for their fact-cramming courses. The tactics they employ more closely resemble supermarkets than schools: flamboyant advertising, discounts and 'specials,' high volume, and quick turnover.

The *cursinhos* are both the cause and effect of many of Brazil's educational problems. Candidates for higher education outnumber available freshman places; the entrance exams serve as the sole basis for admission; and middle-level education fails to prepare students adequately to face the exams. As long as these problems continue to exist, the *cursinhos* will remain a very significant—although illegitimate—part of the Brazilian educational panorama.

Beginning in 1971, the MEC set out to reform, modernize, and equalize the system of access to higher education. Standardized scoring of tests was introduced; the exam content was modified to insure that it corresponded to the knowledge which could reasonably be expected of secondary school graduates. This, it was hoped, would also obviate the candidate's heavy reliance upon a *cursinho*. However, it was only partially successful in this regard.

The entrance exam competition was changed from an eliminatory to a classifying one. In other words, arbitrary passing scores were abolished: if a law school, for example, has 100 freshman places, they would be filled by the candidates with the top 100 scores in the examination competition.

The unification of entrance exams, as recommended in Article 21 of the 1968 University Reform Law, has been adopted on three levels: intra-institutional, inter-institutional (i.e., a consortium of colleges), and regional. The last has been especially noteworthy. To illustrate, CESGRANRIO (Center for the Selection of Candidates to Higher Education in Greater Rio) has offered unified college entrance examinations since 1972 with more than four dozen institutions in Metropolitan Rio de Janeiro participating in the network—public and private; universities and isolated colleges. CESGRANRIO was the model selected by the federal government to be adopted by other geoeducational districts in Brazil.

In São Paulo, the Carlos Chagas Foundation, a privately operated testing and research organization created in 1963 (CESGRANRIO is a *federally* sponsored foundation), conducts the unified entrance examinations for admission to biomedical science programs in Greater São Paulo. Both CESGRANRIO and the Chagas Foundation, as well as other regional testing and research organizations, have developed vocational guidance materials for distribution to candidates prior to the exam registration period. This has alleviated, if nothing else, the tension and apprehension among those sitting for the exams.

Nevertheless, those students who can afford to do so have continued attending *cursinhos* as a precautionary measure.

SOCIAL DEMAND FOR HIGHER EDUCATION

An interesting finding derived by tabulating the 1970 Census data indicates that during college attendance very little earnings need be forgone; in fact, during university attendance earning capacity actually increases beyond high school. Essentially, an education beyond high school pays for itself many times over. The annual growth rate of secondary school graduates has been constant between 1968 and 1972, averaging 13.7 percent per annum. However, the effective demand for higher education has expanded far beyond that percentage (see table 21).

A great part of the demand for higher education is *repressed* demand—those who have delayed applying to college and others

TABLE 21

GROWTH OF CANDIDATES FOR COLLEGE ADMISSION AND NUMBER PASSING THE ENTRANCE EXAMINATIONS: 1960–1975

Year	*Applicants*	*Annual Increase of Applicants (Percent)*	*Cand./ Place*	*Number Passing*	*Proportion Passing (Percent)*
1960	64,637	—	2.7	23,753	36.7
1961	70,147	8.52	2.8	24,705	35.2
1962	70,942	1.13	2.4	29,896	42.1
1963	86,716	22.24	2.3	37,205	42.9
1964	97,481	12.41	2.1	47,219	48.4
1965	110,834	13.70	2.3	48,141	43.4
1966	123,379	11.33	2.4	51,223	41.5
1967	183,150	48.42	2.6	70,915	38.4
1968	214,996	17.39	2.6	82,781	38.5
1969	276,904	28.80	2.5	109,281	39.5
1970	328,931	18.79	2.3	145,000	44.1
1971	400,958	21.90	2.0	202,100	50.4
1972	476,154	18.75	1.8	268,815	56.5
1973	508,615	6.82	1.6	318,028	62.5
1974*	532,477	4.69	1.4	379,098	71.2
1975*	897,022	68.46	2.3	388,000	43.25

* estimates

Source: SEEC (Service for Educational and Cultural Statistics, MEC); DAU (Department of University Affairs, MEC)

who have been unsuccessful in securing admission in previous attempts.

It must be stressed that selection for higher education is mostly *economic* in character. For example, poor students make up a mere 12 percent of the student body at the University of São Paulo. Consequently, student financial aid is essential to satisfy the social demand of lower income students for higher education.

STUDENT FINANCIAL AID

Aside from available outright grants, which inevitably always have fallen far short of demand, a number of projects had been consecutively drawn up by the MEC—without ever getting beyond the planning stage—to provide poor students with the means to obtain a higher education. One recent plan involved the payment of tuition fees by students from well-to-do families in public universities. The monies thus collected were to be put into a rotating scholarship fund for poor students. The plan met with violent opposition from students, professors, and politicians and had to be scrapped.

The breakthrough finally came in 1976 when the federal government launched its Educational Credit Program which is being financed by Brazilian credit institutions. In its initial phase, the program involved 118 institutions of higher education in the North, Northeast, and Center-West of the country, with about 200,000 students. It was estimated that 40,000 of them were in need of financial assistance. In fact, the students' response exceeded by far everyone's expectations. Altogether, 55,665 students applied for financial aid, and 50,253 loans were approved. The plan is now being expanded to the rest of the country.

The Educational Credit Program is being financed with CR$ 10.8 billion between 1976 and 1979. The financing for the 1976 academic year involved CR$ 1.7 billion. The institutions which handle the financial arrangements are the Bank of Brazil, the Federal Savings Bank, and a group of commercial banks. Lending rates are much cheaper than those for commercial loans. The interest rate to the borrower is 15 percent per annum: 12 percent interest charge and 3 percent loan default insurance to be placed in a liquidity fund.

Those students found eligible may choose between two types of loans: (1) full tuition financing for study at a private institution, the money being paid in the student's name directly to the college; and (2) a loan for living expenses and personal maintenance up to a yearly maximum of twelve minimum wages (about CR$ 500 per month) for study at a public higher education institution, the money to be deposited monthly in the student's own bank account.

The terms of repayment specify that one year after graduation the student borrower will begin to repay the loan in monthly installments not to exceed 10 percent of his income.

LABOR MARKET CONDITIONS

The labor market has been excellent for college graduates as a whole—particularly those in the professions. However, dentists and agronomists do earn less than the average university graduate.

By and large, college students are not concerned with market factors in choosing a career. Social status is still most important to Brazilian college students and their families. There are, of course, exceptions. For example, with the soybean boom in the world commodity market, the need for agricultural personnel is great, and agronomy studies are becoming popular in the soybean-producing South, breaking many old social taboos of the middle class.

The first fairly comprehensive study of the national labor market in Brazil was completed in 1972 by the University Research Institute of Rio de Janeiro. It analyzed employment statistics in eight Brazilian states from 1,007 enterprises as well as state and federal organizations. The study projected manpower needs through 1985 for four professions: law, economics, engineering, and business administration. The projections revealed an anticipated oversupply of 40,000 lawyers and 30,000 economists, but possible shortages of 35,000 business administrators and 92,000 engineers. (In Brazil, law school graduates, for the most part, do not practice law; however, they do find decent employment in other areas such as business and public administration; the same holds for economists who also secure suitable jobs in banking, commerce, and management.)

Labor market data of 1976 show the following. *Medicine.* Seventy-three schools will graduate 7,086 new physicians in 1976 and approximately 9,000 in 1977. However, 49 percent remain in the Rio-São Paulo axis following graduation. *Engineering.* If the economy grows at 10 percent per annum and new engineers increase at the same rate, all will find jobs. Otherwise, the poorest prepared engineers will be underemployed, performing duties that could be carried out by technicians with two years of college. *Law.* 18,000 will graduate each year, a 20 percent yearly growth in the stock of lawyers. Only 20 percent who graduate law school actually become practicing attorneys—the rest either never wanted to or cannot make the grade. Most lawyers are badly paid and the majority work in civil law. *Economics and business administration.* In 1964 there were five programs in economics and ten in business administration. Today there are 119 and 192 respectively; over two-thirds are in private institutions. Of the economics graduates, 20 percent practice their profession; for business administration, it is 30 percent. That is all the market can sustain. However, as already mentioned, the rest find well paying jobs in such related areas as public administration, management consulting, and banking.

Unemployment among university graduates is not a serious problem, yet. Frequently, college graduates occupy jobs once held by high school graduates. Not surprising is the fact that the growth in the supply of college graduates has depressed the relative earnings of secondary school graduates. It also appears that the earnings of college graduates are 'administered prices,' tied to social rather than market forces. Consequently, the gap in earnings between university and high school graduates is wide. All economic and social indicators converge to prove that the private benefits obtained from a college degree are great.

TEACHING, RESEARCH, AND GRADUATE EDUCATION

During the past decade, Brazil has sought to upgrade and expand the number of college teachers and researchers and generally improve the quality of graduate education.

While the number of college teachers has grown rapidly since 1964, from 30,872 to 75,931 by 1974, the student-teacher ratio has increased markedly, nevertheless—from 7.4 students per teacher to 11.8 students per teacher. Granted these are comparatively low ratios, it is necessary to point out that the vast majority of college instructors teach part-time. Also, since many teach in more than one institution, they are double-counted. Recent increases in the student-teacher ratio can be attributed, to some extent, to the employment of greater numbers of full-time professors.

In 1974, of 75,931 college professors only 18.73 percent were full-time; 81.27 percent were part-time instructors. Private institutions, especially *faculdades isoladas*, have the highest concentration of part-time faculty.

Since 1969 the Brazilian government has worked to restructure salary and work schedules for professors in federal institutions and has provided financial support and technical assistance to stimulate full-time teaching in public colleges and universities.

In terms of academic credentials, at the beginning of 1975 the teaching body was composed of the following: bachelors degree (53 percent); postgraduate specialist certificate (26.24 percent); masters degree (10.04 percent); and doctorate degree (10.65 percent).

Lack of money has been one of the major reasons for the problem of high level manpower development. Only 15 percent of those who begin masters degree studies actually finish; recognizably only 40 percent of those in the program hold full-time fellowships.

To help correct these deficiencies, the Office of Coordination for the Improvement of Higher Education Personnel (CAPES) and the National Council of Scientific and Technological Development (CNPq) decided in 1975 to appropriate CR$ 600 million beyond their normal funding levels for the 1976–1978 period. CAPES announced in April 1976 that 2,500 professors would take a leave of absence to pursue masters degree studies in Brazil and abroad. Their sponsoring institutions would pay their regular salaries and arrange to hire substitutes to cover the courses of the professors on leave.

In the middle of 1976, the MEC announced that it had projected a need for 40,600 new lecturers by 1979 for undergraduate courses of instruction. In addition to upgraded and new M.A. and Ph.D. degree holders, the country would need a goodly number of highly trained scientific researchers. The government's vehicle for achieving these goals is the *First National Postgraduate Education*

Plan. Approved in mid-1975, the plan will strive to institutionalize graduate education, increase its performance level, and guide and assess its growth. Targets are 16,800 new M.A.s and 1,400 Ph.D.s by 1979, and 1,400 additional degrees awarded to Brazilians pursuing overseas graduate studies. Openings for those seeking a master's degree will increase from 7,000 to 11,700 per year; doctoral program admissions will more than double, from 500 to 1,200. The federal government has set aside CR$ 10.3 billion for the program.

The *Second Basic Plan of Scientific and Technological Development* was also approved in mid-1975. It appropriated CR$ 21 billion for the 1975–1977 period. Several months later President Geisel authorized CR$ 579,083,000 for research projects during the same period, the funds to be spent as follows: part would be allocated to the National Fund for Scientific and Technological Development (FUNTEC), in turn to be dispersed for research activities in fifteen government organizations; and the remaining funds would be assigned to projects under the responsibility of the Ministries of the Army, the Navy, Aeronautics, and the Institute of Space Sciences.

UNIVERSITY EXTENSION

University extension activities in Brazil were developed to create a strong and visible link between higher education and national development. The goals of all extension programs have been fundamentally the same: (1) to provide students with a clearer understanding of regional and national problems and enable them to participate in the nation's development; (2) to encourage students both to apply classroom learning and to acquire skills essential to the country's needs; (3) to tap the university as a development-related resource; and (4) to bring technical assistance and training to Brazil's interior.

The two major vehicles of Brazilian university extension services have been CRUTAC and Projeto Rondon. Together they have provided Brazil with a domestic Peace Corps or, more correctly, VISTA.

CRUTAC was initiated in 1966 in the Federal University of Rio Grande do Norte (UFRN) in Natal. UFRN organized a Rural University Center for Training and Community Action (CRUTAC) in the interior to offer students internships and to provide the rural poor with social and educational services. This orientation, it should be added, is similar to that of the 'land-grant college' idea which emerged in the United States over a century ago.

CRUTACs at the Federal University of Rio Grande do Norte became an integral part of students' senior year of college. For medical students, it counts towards their internship. A unique aspect of CRUTAC is the interdisciplinary nature of the projects undertaken. Multiprofessional teams (e.g., engineers, physicians, teachers, social workers) often collaborate on projects in a number of areas. Some of the major areas in which CRUTAC is involved are: preventive health, sanitary engineering, basic education, nutrition, and juvenile justice.

Today there are twenty-two CRUTACs in federal universities all over Brazil serving the rural population. Interestingly, the Federal University of Minas Gerais has a CRUTAC aimed at providing *urban* extension services. Enterprising universities can, thus, flexibly structure their extension activities; depending upon the area and their collective manpower capacities.

The federal government recognizes CRUTAC as the most important delivery system for university extension services. However, in 1975 the feeling in the DAU was that the expansion of CRUTACs should be temporarily halted; instead, the performance of existing CRUTACs should be evaluated and improved. The federal government's working plan for university extension, issued in 1975, stipulates that the DAU earmark CR$ 14,012,000 for CRUTAC activities for the period 1976–78.

The other major university extension program is Projeto Rondon. It began in 1967 when a university professor from Rio de

Janeiro took a group of twenty-seven student volunteers to help with the development work along a new highway being built in Amazonia. The students gave literacy lessons to local children; helped build bridges; and, in the process, discovered a totally new world.

Projeto Rondon was immediately hailed as a success. Both returning student volunteers and the local communities were enthusiastic. It became a twice-yearly student volunteer vacation program sponsored by the Ministry of the Interior. As a second step, Projeto Rondon fostered nearly two dozen permanent, university-controlled satellite centers known as *campi avançados* (advanced university campuses) in Amazonia. The *campi* are staffed by faculty and students who serve thirty-day tours of duty. The focus of activity depends upon the needs of each particular region; and, unlike CRUTAC, Projeto Rondon has extended its purposes as it has developed.

Since its inception, more than 113,000 students have taken part in Projeto Rondon. Today it has six forms of activities. First, *national operations*. This takes place from January to February when students are sent to different places in the interior all over Brazil. Teams of thirty-two students work in specially selected districts (*municípios*) providing technical assistance and training to develop local infrastructures in these areas. Second is *regional operations* which take place in July in the student's own state or region. Volunteers work in conjunction with local organizations, both public and private, and do whatever work is needed, based upon prior planning. Third, there are the *campi avançados*. Activities in the twenty-three *campi* are as varied as possible and always geared to local needs. Each university participating in the program has chosen its location for a *campus* in accordance with its own manpower capabilities. Fourth, *special operations* can take place any time during the year and usually last about two weeks. They involve such activities as health care and occupational safety, indexing of local archives, and setting up a kindergarten. Fifth, the *interiorization of manpower* program, begun in 1972, pays college graduates to work in the interior for substantial salaries, for a year, for half-day work. Work conditions can be shocking for professionals coming from the cities, and without a decent wage, it would be impossible to attract professionals. Sixth, there are *paid work stages*. Over the years, Projeto Rondon has become somewhat of an employment agency for future professionals. State and local government and other large organizations which are inadequately staffed to carry out particular work assignments will request that Projeto Rondon send them students for half-time work. A good example is INPS, the federal social security administration which in 1975 employed 11,000 students screened by Projeto Rondon.

Although service in Projeto Rondon does *not* carry credit towards a student's professional course of study, it does fulfill part of the basic course requirements in civics—compulsory from first-level through third-level schooling.

In December 1975, Projeto Rondon became a foundation. Its aim is to motivate growing numbers of Brazilian university students to take part voluntarily in the processes of national development and integration. The Foundation's projected goal for 1977 was 100,000 participants. 'Foundation' status enables Projeto Rondon to receive some of its funding directly out of the federal budget. Partial funding for 1976 amounted to CR$ 120 million (U.S.$ 10 million) resulting in part from transfers of funds and donations. The Foundation's initial goal was to increase the number of participants in Projeto Rondon operations to 100,000 a year.

AMAZONIAN STUDIES

Brazil is a tropical country, but what might be called its 'tropical' education is of quite recent date. Most of the network of tropical research and training programs now being implemented in Amazonia are the direct outgrowth of Brazilian government efforts after 1970 to integrate the enormous Amazon region into the rest of the nation. At the start of the vast Trans-Amazonian road building program, concerned Brazilians and international scientists vehemently criticized the fact that the program had not been preceded by thorough and lengthy studies dealing with the areas suddenly opened up by the new roads. Even after 350 years of European occupancy, the region's ecology, historical processes, population patterns, social organization, natural resources, and economic potential remain largely unknown.

New multifaceted study-and-training programs are today being organized in Amazonia to study these questions, while training experts capable of tackling the problems of a rapidly changing tropical region. One of the institutes trying to cut with solid scientific research through the lush mythology enshrouding Brazilian Amazonia is the Nucleus of Postgraduate Amazonian Studies (NAEA) at the Federal University of Pará, in Belém.

NAEA started its work in February 1973 with an 'international program in regional development training' open to qualified college graduates from Brazil, from five other Pan-Amazonian nations (Venezuela, Colombia, Equador, Peru and Bolivia), and from Africa. NAEA's basic goal is the training of personnel able to identify, analyze, interpret and, it is hoped, help solve the problems of the Amazonian regions, particularly in their socioeconomic and technical aspects. In other words, NAEA aims to produce the expert manpower whose lack has so far thwarted all attempts at rational regional development.

For the next few years, NAEA's training program will focus on regional economy, human resources, and ecology. A student spends half of his class hours on group research in the 'research laboratory' where he works on a specific research project with four or five other students from different disciplines. He must complete sixty-three credits to graduate as a 'Specialist in Regional Development' and then can, if he wishes, go on to complete his studies for a masters degree in development planning.

NAEA's admissions criteria are both stringent and realistic. Aside from submitting the usual academic credentials and study projects, a candidate must be 'highly motivated for postgraduate studies.' He must also be able to convince the admissions committee of his intention to stay in the region and to continue working in activities related to Amazonian development.

NAEA is Brazil's first Amazonian research institute to operate as part of a university, and at the postgraduate level. Since the development of research in Brazil started at the turn of the century and thus antedates the creation of universities, Brazilian research, most of it 'applied' or problem oriented, has remained the nearly exclusive domain of scientific institutes not linked to any university.

Brazilian Amazonia today has a handful of specifically tropical research institutes. The oldest and most prestigious is the Goeldi Museum in Belém which was founded by the Swiss naturalist Emile Goeldi; research at the Goeldi Museum focuses on natural sciences, ethnology, anthropology and archeology. A more recent but by now perhaps equally well-known institute is the National Institute for Amazonian Research (INPA) in Manaus, with its work in environmental sciences, tropical botany, forest research, tropical pathology, phytochemistry, et al. INPA's 'Intensive Training Program for Work in the Amazon' antedates that of NAEA by three years. INPA's program lasts six months and combines the study of Amazonian ecology and tropical hygiene with a solid systemic groundwork in statistics, research methodology, and general laboratory techniques. Here, too, students must be college graduates and give proof of their serious intent to continue working in Amazonia on problems related to its development. Since 1975 INPA has offered a master's degree in tropical botany.

Institutes such as Goeldi Museum and INPA are today assisting the Amazonian universities in setting up their special regional studies programs. The Federal University of Pará in Belém is, as has been noted, the first university to organize such a program at the postgraduate level. The Federal University of Mato Grosso in Cuiabá has totally oriented its undergraduate courses towards the acquisition of knowledge about the Amazon region, with particular stress on health and community programs for the surrounding indigenous population (the university is today known in Brazil as 'The University of the Jungle'). The Federal University of Amazonas in Manaus has started courses in Amazonian technology.

7
Nonformal Education

PARALLEL forms of instruction outside the traditional school system are provided by Brazil's *Ensino Supletivo* (supplementary instruction). Some of these parallel courses are geared for young people who failed to complete their schooling at the appropriate age levels but would like to catch up at a later date; many of these youngsters are getting another chance at going back into the regular school system through intensive courses, and *exames supletivos* (equivalency exams). Other courses give industrial, commercial, or agricultural training to working youngsters and adults. A broad, and in part anonymous, audience of all ages is reached nationwide by radio and television courses which also permit participants to sit for *exames supletivos*. Added to that is MOBRAL, Brazil's famous mass literacy movement, which started out as a simple drive to stamp out illiteracy among Brazilian adults but has gradually branched out into a variety of community-oriented educational and cultural programs.

Not including MOBRAL students, it is estimated that more than five million Brazilians take part in nonformal education programs.

All of these parallel forms of instruction, some of which have existed for several decades, have been regulated by Law no. 5,692 so as to form an educational subsystem, linked to the school structure but with the flexibility needed to make of education a lifelong learning process.

EXAMES SUPLETIVOS

Exames supletivos, the former '*exames de madureza*,' are held at two levels: as equivalency of first-level school graduation for youngsters over eighteen, and of second-level school graduation for youngsters over twenty-one. In 1975, 2,625,161 candidates sat for *exames supletivos* all over Brazil; their core contingent came from the so-called *suplência* courses (the former *cursos de madureza*), both public and private, which correspond to first- and second-school instruction and are in demand mainly in urban areas. (See table 22.)

TABLE 22

EXAMES SUPLETIVOS—1975

Region	First-Level *Candidates*	First-Level *Approvals*	Second-Level *Candidates*	Second-Level *Approvals*
South	55,503	20,188	80,496	23,082
Southeast	839,574	289,072	913,137	315,396
Centereast	110,282	33,966	155,653	42,762
Northeast	216,380	81,998	189,443	66,239
North	28,319	13,122	36,374	13,353
	1,250,058	438,346	1,375,103	460,832

Total number of candidates: 2,625,161
Total number of approvals: 899,178

Source: MEC/DESU

The entire examinations process is slowly being streamlined nationwide. During the so-called golden era of *madureza* exams, before 1969, the federal education system authorized private schools in different cities to organize paid tests and to issue diplomas. Needless to say, the standards of those tests varied widely, as did the inscription fees, if in an inverse ratio. Often thousands of candidates from all points of the country converged on a small town in the interior where a private school organized easy tests, to be rewarded with outrageous inscription fees.

The responsibility for *supletivo* exams has now gone over to the states. The exams may still be held in public as well as private schools, but only with permission from the State Education Secretariat which is fully responsible for the tenor of the exams.

The 1971 Law has also made possible the creation of new *cursos supletivos seriados*, which teach the full first-level and second-level school curricula in half the time needed in regular school and may themselves test and graduate their students. In 1975, 800,000 students attended these *cursos* in Rio de Janeiro and São Paulo.

The *cursos supletivos seriados* are included in the MEC's new '*Estratégia Nacional do Ensino Supletivo*' elaborated in 1976; the plan aims to eliminate the *supletivo* exams (table 22) entirely and to create a modern nationwide system of public *cursos supletivos* with nontraditional teaching methods which will progressivly evaluate their students and distribute certificates.

But for some years at least, *supletivo* students will still have to sit for exams. Their approval rate as a rule has been less than 40 percent and in 1975 was only 34.3 percent. Yet in spite of all the odds against them, students who pass the second-level school graduation equivalency seem to have a relatively fair, if inevitably slim, chance at university admission. In Rio's unified *vestibulares* for 1975, 22 percent of the candidates who said they had passed *supletivo* exams gained admission to higher education, as against approval rate of 30 percent of the candidates who had graduated from regular second-level school (see table 23).

And like their colleagues from the regular school system, candidates for second-level *supletivo* exams dream of entering a liberal profession and gaining professional prestige. According to a survey conducted in São Paulo in 1973, *supletivo* students, whatever their background and that of their often poor families, usually have a traditional view of their perspectives. The survey found that candidates for *supletivo* exams usually returned to school after a long interval, to pursue goals they had cherished for a long time and which, as a rule, *were totally unrelated to their occupations of the moment*. Nor were they linked to labor market conditions, but rather to the students' notions of social prestige based on traditional concepts. Thus, the majority of those interviewed mentioned only

TABLE 23

DISTRIBUTION OF CANDIDATES AND CLASSIFICATIONS ACCORDING TO ORIGIN OF SECOND-LEVEL SCHOOL GRADUATION CERTIFICATES IN FUNDAÇÃO CESGRANRIO 1975 UNIVERSITY ADMISSION EXAMS

Origin of Second-Level School Graduation Certificate	*Number of Candidates*	*Percent*	*Classifications*	*Percent*
Exames Supletivos	9,167	12.0	1,977	22.0
Regular School	66,181	88.0	20,006	30.0
Total	75,348	100.00	21,983	29.0

Source of Data: Fundação CESGRANRIO, as quoted in '*Relação entre a Aprovação nos Exames Supletivos de 2° Grau e a Promoção nos Exames Vestibulares.*' Cláudio de Moura Castro; PUC/INEP, Rio de Janeiro 1976

twelve professions as desirable, nearly all of them traditional. Most frequently cited were medicine, engineering, and law.

Tailored for a far more realistic clientele is the recently instituted *Exame Supletivo Professionalizante*, which puts an official seal of approval on professional qualifications gained by persons without proper schooling. A survey made in Minas Gerais and São Paulo, Brazil's most industrialized states, showed that 66 percent of the industrial employees with technical jobs had not graduated from regular schools. The *exame supletivo professionalizante* was thus created to evaluate, officially, professional abilities after they have, in fact, been recognized by employers. A candidate for these exams need not be twenty-one and, if approved, will get a certificate of second-level *técnico*.

SENAI, SENAC, PIPMO

Professional training, for youngsters and adults with or without proper schooling, is provided chiefly by the *Serviço Nacional de Aprendizagem Industrial*—National Industrial Training Service—(SENAI) and the *Serviço Nacional de Aprendizagem Comercial*—National Commercial Training Service—(SENAC), two privately maintained programs, and the *Programa Intensive de Preparação de*

Mão-de-Obra—Intensive Manpower Training Program—(PIPMO), a federal program which has recently moved from the orbit of the MEC to that of the Ministry of Labor.

SENAI was created in 1942. With its apprenticeship, training, and professional specialization programs, SENAI was the precursor of similar programs elsewhere in Latin America (SENA, Colombia; CONED, Argentina; SENATI, Peru; INSE, Venezuela; INACAP, Chile) and of Great Britain's Industrial Training Act of 1963.

SENAI is a private organization administered by the National Confederation of Industries, and maintained by a 1 percent voluntary payroll tax contributed by Brazil's industrial, transportation, communications and fishing enterprises. Its first adult training courses were created under pressure for industrial mobilization during World War II.

SENAI's chief activities today are: (1) the training of industrial manpower through its apprenticeship courses for youngsters between fourteen and eighteen; (2) intensive professional training for employed and unemployed adults; and (3) retraining and specialization courses for qualified workers and supervisors. Added to that is a whole gamut of courses of varied duration for industrial personnel at all levels. More than half of SENAI's courses are given at its own centers. The rest are given at factory sites.

In its thirty-four years of operation SENAI has reached close to four million workers (including 830,000 youngsters), of whom 75 percent were trained after 1968, i.e. propelled by Brazil's latest industrial development spurt.

SENAC was created in 1946, on the same principles as SENAI, to provide training for commercial and service occupations. SENAC offers courses for about 90 different occupations, at its more than 100 training centers all over Brazil, and through on-the-job training courses in large commercial enterprises. For example, with Brazil's new efforts to attract tourists from abroad and offer them accommodations with internationally acceptable standards, the training of hotel and restaurant personnel has become a priority endeavor. Thus, SENAC operates its own restaurants to train cooks, waiters and barmen. In São Paulo which, of course, has Brazil's most diversified and sophisticated training facilities, SENAC funds (again, the voluntary 1 percent payroll tax contributed by employers) maintain professional training centers and mobile units, as well as a 'school hotel,' a 'pedagogic supermarket,' 'school-luncheonettes,' and a model store-office. In thirty years, SENAC has trained more than 1 million persons for commercial and service jobs.

The *Programa Intensivo de Preparação de Mão-de-Obra*—Intensive Manpower Training Program—(PIPMO), a federal program was originally started as an industrial training program, PIPMOI, in 1963, as a result of the need to upgrade the skills of labor employed in the industrial sector. In 1969 the program was expanded to train also workers in the tertiary and primary sectors, in urban and rural areas, and three years later branched out into a special project to provide intensive training for unemployed rural and urban youth. From 1964 to 1976, PIPMO has trained more than one million workers in all three sectors.

Different from SENAI and SENAC, PIPMO is a funding and coordinating agency, which lays out its projects according to local needs and then contracts labor unions, private concerns and vocational schools to execute its programs. Also, until early 1976, PIPMO remained the only agency to train rural workers who constituted about one-third of its 450,000 trainees in 1975.

Thus, of the 1,250,000 workers trained by SENAI, SENAC, and PIPMO in 1975, only 150,000 were rural workers, a sharp imbalance in terms of manpower training—and of social development—since rural workers account for 44.3 percent of Brazil's labor force.

(It should be mentioned here that the Brazilian Constitution permits children to work once they are twelve years old, but that labor legislation has put a series of restrictions on the employment of youngsters under fourteen. Nevertheless, the term 'labor force'—fully employed, partially employed, underemployed—statistically refers to Brazilians *ten years old and up*. For example, a 1975 government survey showed that in 1972 and 1973 the participation of ten- to fourteen-year-olds in the Brazilian labor force grew by 15 percent. The share of fifteen- to nineteen-year-olds grew by 9 percent and, together, the two age-groups accounted for more than one-third of the labor force expansion in those two years.)

To push the much-needed training of rural workers, a federal program called *Serviço Nacional de Formação Professional Rural*—National Service for Professional Rural Training—(SENAR), was created in 1976 within the Labor Ministry to train an additional 700,000 rural workers by 1979.

RADIO AND TELEVISION EDUCATION

Since October 1970, all Brazilian commercial radio and television stations must broadcast, free of charge, at least one hour of educational programs each day. Most states further operate their own educational radio stations or *TV Cultura* channels (and, in some cases, both), which usually operate for a few hours a day and serve a variety of purposes: to broadcast educational programs produced by the MEC, or by other states (usually São Paulo or Rio), as well as special cultural, musical, and sports programs, and courses of community interest.

Up to mid 1976, the MEC not only produced or sponsored programs, but also operated its own two radio stations and one educational television station. With the creation of Radiobrás, the federal mass communications agency under the Ministry of Communications, the MEC lost its stations but remained as the producer of educational-cultural programs through its *Serviço de Radiodifusão Educativa* in Brasília, and the first of its television production centers, the *Fundação Centro Brasileiro de TV Educativa* (FCBTVE) in Rio. The MEC is further supposed to come up with a national 'policy' and to 'coordinate' the plethora of educational radio and television programs all over Brazil. In the eyes of most experts, they constitute a patchwork of spottily successful (or unsuccessful) projects still far from doing justice to the enormous educational potential of mass media.

PROJETO MINERVA

The most important among the more than two dozen educational radio programs—state, regional, and national—is Projeto Minerva, a federal program created in 1970. It is estimated that in the first three years of its existence it reached 250,000 students of all ages, who gathered for its '*Supletivo Dinâmico*' (an eight months' course equivalent to grades one through four) at 6,000 'radioposts' all over Brazil. In 1974, about 100,000 students completed the second phase of '*Supletivo Primeiro Gráu*' (grades five through eight; duration thirteen months).

As a rule, a group of about thirty students provided with free mimeographed instruction sheets sits around a radio in a community meeting hall. Classes five days a week consist of fifteen-minute radio lessons, complemented by the explanations of a trained monitor. On Saturdays, there is an hour's revision class. Each batch of leaflets is good for a month of classes. The same leaflets can also be bought by anyone who wants to follow radio classes at home, and who can then sit for tests just like the officially registered students.

The cost to the MEC per registered student, for the eight months' *Supletivo Dinâmico*, has been figured at about thirty-five dollars, including the free distribution of instruction sheets.

In 1975, Projeto Minerva had 400,000 registered students, but the number of students receiving diplomas at the end of their respective courses has remained relatively modest and hovers at about 30 percent of those registered.

FUNDAÇÃO PADRE ANCHIETA

A striking example of the potential, in both efficiency and cost, of mass media education was provided by São Paulo State's education and television center, *Fundação Padre Anchieta*, only a year after its programs first went on the air. Its students were found to perform better in *madureza* exams than their colleagues from *supletivo* (i.e., *suplência*) classes, and at a fraction of the cost to the state of students in regular schools.

In November 1970, 42,867 students registered for São Paulo's eighth-grade *madureza* exams (today's first-level *exames supletivos*, at the time called *madureza ginasial*). They included, for the first time, candidates who had prepared themselves through the Fundação's 'intensive' radio and television instruction equivalent to grades five through eight. When test results and registration data were sifted at the end of the exams, it turned out that of the 13,004 candidates prepared via radio and television, 6,477 had passed, i.e., an approval rate of 49.8 percent, as against an approval rate of only 40 percent (11,960 students) among the 29,863 candidates from *suplência* classes. Furthermore, each of the Fundação's graduates cost the state only about ten dollars. In regular public school, for example, the cost per student in grades five through eight would have been seventy-five dollars a year.

Fundação Padre Anchieta, well-funded, with a wide gamut of educational, cultural, and artistic programs based on nearly two years of research and tests, remains for most experts Brazil's best mass media education project. Its nonformal instruction programs were rapidly adopted for broadcasting by other Brazilian states.

TV Cultura, São Paulo, today broadcasts eighteen hours of programs a day, half of them devoted to education and the other half to cultural subjects.

OVERVIEW OF EDUCATIONAL TELEVISION PROGRAMS

Sesame Street, the world's best-known and most widely adapted television preschool education program, was also adapted in Brazil, as '*Vila Sésamo.*' Its locale was transposed from an inner-city ghetto in the United States to Bela Vista, a run-down, former middle-class neighborhood in São Paulo, where Gugu (the Cookie Monster) and Garibaldi (Big Bird) helped by amiable neighbors named Juca, Anamaria, and Seu Almeida played hosts to ever-changing groups of small children. Following the first closed-circuit test projections in August 1972, *Vila Sésamo* was broadcast in São Paulo by *TV Cultura* as of October 1972.

Newspaper reports say that the program's first 130 episodes were received with equal enthusiasm by children and adults. But there has been little other than these newspaper reports. No funds were made available to assess the program's scholastic results and the size and type of the audiences reached by it, or to make any other kind of evaluation.

Since the programming of additional sections of *Vila Sésamo* will have to be preceded by a thorough evaluation of all its aspects, *TV Cultura* so far has had to continue repeating its transmissions of the first section, over and over again, and rather into the blue.

Aside from this limited attempt at preschool education, Brazilian educational television today consists of two types: the *supletivo*, aimed at about fifteen million Brazilians over eighteen who have not attended school at the proper time, and regular classroom instruction to supplement the insufficient and generally inadequate schools in Brazil's poor rural areas. Educational television projects of either type, with programs at different educational levels, and with inevitably varied rates of efficiency, have proliferated all over Brazil.

To name at random just a few, there is, for example, the *TVE Rio Grande do Sul*, a state project originally intended to give both *supletivo* and formal instruction. Because of various initial snafus, it took nearly five years to start operations and so far broadcasts mostly programs in 'support' of formal classroom instruction if in a broad range of subjects (mathematics and science, grades five through seven; German, French and English, grades nine through eleven, et al).

The *TVE Universitária de Recife*, run by the Federal University of Pernambuco, started broadcasting in 1968, as one of the links in the Pan-American educational television network. Its programs, some of them excellent, have ranged from literacy courses to a university-level course in anatomy. Admittedly, the project has no overall plan and suffers from 'lack of definition.'

Many of the state educational television projects suffer from 'lack of definition.' Most of them suffer from lack of funds. When programs are brought in from São Paulo, as is frequent, their contents may jar with the regional culture; or, as has happened at one northeastern television center, the two-inch tapes from Rio will not fit the local equipment if that has been imported from Europe. But in spite of all that, there are at least two state educational television stations which are excellent: that of Minas Gerais (TVE-MG), and the one of Maranhão (FMTE).

Minas Gerais is a state geoeconomically divided in two: its northern half is an extension of Brazil's underdeveloped Northeast. Its southern half, with some of Latin America's largest mining and foundry industries, is part of Brazil's industrialized center-south.

TVE-MG has started with *supletivo* programs, concentrating on professionalizing courses. Its main goal is the professionalization of youngsters between fifteen and nineteen, of whom only 12 percent are in school. For example, an open-circuit course in business administration lasting eighteen weeks is being broadcast to groups at SENAI, SENAC, the Institute of Education, and other educational centers, Another course, in reading and interpreting technical designs, is being broadcast to workers and factories where television posts have been installed. Up to now, the programs are limited to greater Belo Horizonte, the capital, with a population of about two million. If the state can find the funds—there seems to be no shortage of expert technical help—this type of educational television will be expanded to reach the rest of the state. TVE-MG is, by any standards, a 'modest' operation. But it has that vital thing, 'direction.'

The same goes for FMTE, the *Fundação Maranhense de Televisão*, which has endeavored, successfully, to make up for an underdeveloped state's grievous lack of schools with television classroom instruction. FMTE is a grassroots project. It was developed by two *maranhense* educators who wanted to tackle what they saw as the state's most serious educational problem: a virtual void in public education after the first four grades. According to 1970 census figures, only about 10 percent of Maranhão's eligible age group was matriculated in grades five through eight.

FMTE started operating in 1969 in São Luis, Maranhão's capital, with a few hundred students. Today its telecenters in São Luis, Ribamar and Passo do Luminar, two towns in the interior, teach the full programs of grades five through eight, i.e., both academic and vocational courses, to close to 15,000 students. The students, attending classes under the supervision of monitors, most of whom are college graduates, have four lessons daily, each consisting of twenty minutes of television instruction followed by thirty minutes of work around a problem given at the end of the television presentation. There are homework, group activities, museum visits, science projects—all of them oriented around the carefully constructed television lessons. Programs remain flexible and subject to continuing improvement, based on feedback from the students; there are practically no drop-outs, and 98 percent of FMTE's students are passing in final exams.

FMTE's type of education—schooling but with modern techniques and modern curricula and, most important, totally devoid of traditional stuffiness—has been called trendsetting for other state projects; it has already served as a model for educational television in Amazonas, Piauí and Ceará. FMTE has the plans, but so far neither the money nor the facilities, to extend its operations to the rest of Maranhão.

Brazil's most ambitious educational television projects—one formal, the other nonformal—were expected to grow to national scope, but are stalled. Both of them will have to be reformulated before they can have the anticipated impact on Brazilian education.

PROJETO SACI

Sistema Avançado de Comunicações Interdisciplinares (SACI), a project for mass education via satellite, is the child, both technically and pedagogically, of Brazil's Institute of Space Research (INPE) in São Paulo, and specifically of its director, Fernando Mendonça, a space engineer of world renown.

It is conceivable that if Fernando Mendonça's efforts had been successful, SACI might have solved the problem of fragmentation, rivalry, and duplication in the conventional educational television network programs. But Mendonça could not get the government to underwrite an expensive satellite education system. Brazil expects to start operating its first communications satellite by 1981 or so but, in all likelihood, will not use it for educational purposes since they can be adequately, and far more cheaply, served by Brazil's rapidly expanding and still underutilized microwave network.

Also, soon after Projeto SACI started broadcasting its formal basic education courses in 1972 in Rio Grande do Norte, via closed-circuit television, it turned out that its programs, which had been produced by experts in São Paulo with great care, clashed with the local culture of one of Brazil's poorest states. The chief value of Projeto SACI so far has been that it has created an efficient method of training non-qualified teachers for television classroom instruction. The program's pedagogic components are at present under revision.

FCBTVE

Fundação Centro Brasileiro de Televisão Educativa (FCBTVE) is the organization which owns and operates some of Brazil's most sophisticated television equipment. FCBTVE was equipped with a US$ 2·5 million grant from the Konrad Adenauer Foundation. It developed a nonformal education serial, a *telenovela* consisting of 100 thirty-minute chapters which condense the first four grades of first-level school into five-and-a-half months' instruction.

The *telenovela*, called 'João da Silva', started being broadcast in November 1973 over 306 *telepostos* in Rio de Janeiro to about

12,000 adults. The experts who prepared the chapters said that each segment contained about 30 percent of purely 'pedagogic' material whose preparation took up more than 70 percent of the time allotted for production.

In 1974, João da Silva's evaluation tests (i.e., *exames supletivos*) approved 43 percent of the candidates who presented themselves for exams. The ratio was considered excellent since these students accomplished in five months what formal school does in four years (and *cursos supletivos seriados* in two years).

In 1975, 'João da Silva' was being transmitted to ten states. FCBTVE, however, has attempted to remain an 'independent' operation and endeavored to impress its policies on the MEC, instead of vice versa. Today, its production facilities are considered of far greater value than its educational potential; it is therefore likely that FCBTVE will be incorporated into the Ministry of Communications and function merely as a production center for television programs, both educational and general.

MOBRAL (FUNDAÇÃO MOVIMENTO BRASILEIRO DE ALFABETIZAÇÃO)

Structure and scope MOBRAL, Brazil's literacy movement, can perhaps best be described by explaining first what it is not: MOBRAL is not one of the functional literacy projects which are coupled with specific vocational training and aimed at selected groups; nor is it based on lengthy, sophisticated, and often expensive curricula development as has been the case with projects tested, usually with UNESCO support, in well-defined 'pilot' areas of different developing countries. MOBRAL is a mass movement, organized without particularly innovative teaching methods but with a new and highly efficient system of operation, flexible, informal, and unbureaucratic, which enabled it to reach 19.5 million illiterates all over Brazil from 1970 to mid- 1975 of whom, according to official statistics, eight million became literate (see table 24) at a cost per student of about nine U.S. dollars.

TABLE 24

NUMBER OF ILLITERATES IN BRAZIL, WITH FIGURES FROM TWO OFFICIAL SOURCES: IBGE AND MOBRAL

	IBGE	*Percent*	*MOBRAL*	*Percent*
1940	13,280,000	56.2	—	—
1950	15,272,000	50.5	—	—
1960	15,816,000	39.4	—	—
1970	18,147,701	33.6	—	—
1971	—	—	17,213,850	30.9
1972	14,088,105	26.7	14,059,636	26.7
1973	14,293,556	24.2	14,042,868	23.8
1974	—	—	12,455,685	20.5
1975	—	—	11,763,153	18.7

RESULTS ACHIEVED BETWEEN 1970 AND 1974 IN THE FUNCTIONAL LITERACY PROGRAM

	Students	*Graduates*
1970	510,340	169,434
1971	2,569,862	1,093,066
1972	4,284,612	2,016,000
1973	4,920,000	1,722,000
1974	4,760,000	1,951,000
1975 (1° semester)	2,427,371	1,211,500
TOTAL	19,472,185	8,163,000

Jornal do Brasil, Rio de Janeiro; 7 September 1975

MOBRAL has given technical assistance with literacy campaigns to five countries (Senegal, Jamaica, Colombia, Bolivia, and Paraguay) and has been requested to do so by nine others.

Starting with its five-months adult literacy courses, elaborated at MOBRAL's national center but implemented throughout Brazil's cities and rural townships with the help of intelligently mobilized community groups, MOBRAL has fulfilled an important function by helping build solid local bases, nationwide, on which further programs of nonformal education can establish their work.

Literacy courses are followed by the monthly distribution of *Jornal do MOBRAL*, a publication tailored to the intellectual horizon of newly literates. MOBRAL 'graduates' can enroll in specially created 'integrated' courses of further education. MOBRAL has created vocational training courses, organized employment centers and cultural posts, and has sent mobile libraries called *Mobraltecas* around the country. As of 1974, MOBRAL worked on a project to catch the masses of Brazilian school-dropouts between nine and fourteen before they could turn into 'adult' illiterates, to make them literate in special courses tailored to juvenile horizons, and then to send them back to regular school.

It is perhaps not surprising that this last endeavor should finally have triggered an explosion among traditionalists opposed to MOBRAL's growing 'parallel education empire.' First, a Senator in the Congressional Education Commission denounced MOBRAL's new project as 'unconstitutional.' His denunciations were reinforced practically overnight by an array of educators accusing MOBRAL of encroaching on the territory reserved for the regular education establishment. This in turn led to the claim that funds allocated to MOBRAL could be put to far better use in regular education, since no one could prove that people made literate by MOBRAL in fact remained literate and that, in the final analysis, MOBRAL had achieved little else than to act as a sop for Brazilians concerned about the state of their education.

A Parliamentary Investigation Commission (CPI) was instituted in October 1975 as a result of the snowballing protests; it came up with its report in May 1976. The report has been called a whitewash by MOBRAL's detractors since it is a bland, factual, and neutral document. In essence, the CPI report mainly summarizes MOBRAL's activities to date which, for an unbiased observer, continue to represent an achievement of unprecedented scope.

Bases and working methods Illiteracy is an old enemy in Brazil. In 1940, more than thirteen million adult Brazilians, 56.2 percent of Brazil's population over fifteen, were illiterate. While over the next three decades the proportion of illiterates decreased to 33.6 percent, their continuing increase in absolute numbers was in part owing to a system of education which failed to keep step with population growth. By 1970, Brazil had more than eighteen million adult illiterates. (See table 24.)

MOBRAL was created by the 'Functional Literacy and Continuing Education Plan for Adolescents and Adults,' decreed in 1967 and succeeding a string of literacy plans, drives, and movements. None of them had ever gotten off the ground. Sporadic private literacy programs in different regions as a rule had lacked both organization and funds. An adult literacy program organized as part of MEB, the *Movimento de Educação de Base* (Basic Education Movement) sponsored by the Brazilian Roman Catholic church and referring to 'social justice' in some of its teaching material, was seen as highly 'subversive' after 1964 and thus suppressed. And the famous adult literacy program conceived by the Brazilian educator Paulo Freire, the 'psycho-social method,' which aims to make poor people literate while also preparing them to break out of their social, economic, and political marginalization, was considered as anathema by the military regime, and every vestige of it extirpated.

MOBRAL's activities, too, remained marginal for nearly three years mainly through lack of money and organization. In 1970, proper funding, pervasive government propaganda, and complete decentralization turned the former stepchild of educational bureaucracies into a nationwide drive with community involvement. 'No other service agency, not even the telephone or the mails, succeeded in penetrating Brazil's remotest areas the way MOBRAL did,' says the CPI report.

The 1967 Literacy Plan set a series of tasks to attend to the illiterates of different age groups. (One of those prescribed tasks was the 'educational assistance' to illiterate youngsters between ten and fourteen.) But MOBRAL's drive was to limit itself, if one can say so, to providing literacy courses for Brazil's illiterates between fifteen and thirty-five, and only in urban areas for its first year of operation.

It was clear from the start that with Brazil's chronic shortage of qualified teachers the thousands of instructors needed for MOBRAL classes would have to be recruited among unqualified rural teachers, high-school students, and simply local citizens willing to go through intensive training, and to accept MOBRAL's fee of less than three U.S. dollars for each pupil continuing beyond the fourth month. (MOBRAL teachers are not paid per 'graduate,' for obvious reasons, but instead for each student they have brought close to completion of the course.)

How MOBRAL can mobilize a community can be seen by its activities in Abaetetuuba, a town in the state of Pará near the Amazon. In 1971, the young President of the Municipal Commission asked the town's primary and high school students to bring him names and addresses of illiterates. Pupils were then gathered in twenty-five literacy posts, most of which had first to be provided with water and electricity to make them usable. Various inducements were given to the pupils: movie-tickets and bus-rides at half price; free medical and dental care through a 'special' Public Health Service. As a result, literacy classes passed the critical halfway mark with only 32 dropouts out of an initial matriculation of 1,325 pupils. 'Student cards,' with whatever privileges they may entail in the different localities, are today given to pupils in literacy classes everywhere.

Some townships have been harder to mobilize and, in the beginning, met MOBRAL's organizers with passive resistance. Since literacy is a prerequisite for voting in Brazil, provincial mayors feared the possible impact of newly enfranchised poor on local governments. In the 1974 state and federal elections, about five million former illiterates over eighteen were able to go to the polls for the first time.

A MOBRAL coordinator in Pernambuco, one of the states in Brazil's poor Northeast, quotes as the typical reaction among the foremen of the large sugar plantations there: 'A literate worker gives nothing but trouble.' As a rule, literacy students in rural areas are workers who come to classes after a heavy day's work in the fields, are weak and undernourished, and follow instruction only with difficulty. Many are migrant workers who are unable, or unwilling, to stay with a course for more than a few weeks. Brazil's rural areas have 45 percent of its adult population and 68 percent of its illiterates.

Cost and value Following the first euphoria about the millions of illiterates all over Brazil going to MOBRAL classes and becoming literate by the hundreds of thousands, the entire operation was sharply criticized from various angles: that the dropout rate was high, particularly in rural areas; that the proportion of MOBRAL 'graduates,' overall, came to little more than 40 percent; that many pupils who finished the course had not really learned how to read and write; and that literacy remained evanescent, and anyway of little practical use, among poor people living in Brazil's rural hinterlands. And, insistently, the claim that MOBRAL, an operation aimed at redeeming adults, was extravagantly funded in a country which needed every available penny to organize proper education for its children. As one Federal Deputy said before the CPI, MOBRAL was a 'salesman of illusions,' and a 'total economic waste.'

In five years, MOBRAL has cost approximately US$130 million, with funds coming about equally from its share in the National Sports Lottery, and from federal income tax. (In February 1976, the permissible 1 percent income tax deduction for contribution to MOBRAL was increased to 2 percent.) Two-thirds of MOBRAL's funds have been spent on literacy classes; the rest has gone into MOBRAL's '*educação integrada*' (which covers in one year the first four grades of first-level education), administration, and cultural projects.

What is the true value of a mass literacy movement, in the long run? Until the end of 1975, no large-scale evaluation had been undertaken on possible regression rates. One spot test, made in the interior of Pernambuco in 1973, found that 80 percent of a group of newly literate rural workers had forgotten how to write less than a year after 'graduation.' But, as one Brazilian commented: 'Never mind the regression rate, particularly since that will vary so widely from place to place. Those people have been neglected all their lives; they never had a chance at getting an education. The government owes it to them to make at least the attempt to turn them into citizens.'

In all probability, what is 'wrong' with MOBRAL is not that it has failed, but rather that it has succeeded too well and that an overwhelming number of new literates, mainly young people between fifteen and twenty, are now making demands for further education with which regular education is simply unable to cope. Thus, MOBRAL's growing 'parallel education empire.'

Extended goals MOBRAL's *Educação Integrada* started with a 'pilot' program for 34,000 students in 1971. In 1974, out of nearly 2 million new literates from the 1973 contingent, 1.1 million could go on to *educação integrada* classes. A program of technical and professional education which started in 1973 with 40,000 students is expanding as fast as facilities and teachers can be organized. All over the country 1,076 cultural posts have been set up with radio programs, popular art, folklore, painting and music groups, and libraries to prevent regression among those who have learned to read and write. The six *Mobraltecas* which are slowly touring the country serve the same purpose on a mobile basis. Each *Mobralteca* has 2,000 books, musical instruments, a small stage, and closed circuit television.

Where MOBRAL went astray—at least, in Brazilian contexts—was with the projected program for schoolage children: *Programa Nacional de Recuperação de Excedentes* (called initially *MOBRAL Infanto-Juvenil*). This project had in fact two roots. One was the age span of pupils in literacy classes. While they were supposed to teach only illiterates over fifteen, in practice it was found that many under fifteen slipped in, too. MOBRAL's statistics showed that for the years 1972 and 1973 combined, 18.3 percent of all its literacy students, nationwide, were between nine and fourteen, with the largest ratio—more than 25 percent—in the Northeast (see table 25).

TABLE 25

Sample 1972 – 400,000 students
1973 – 1,360,000 students

DISTRIBUTION OF MOBRAL STUDENTS BY AGE GROUPS
(Percent)

	Region	*9–14*	*15–25*	*26–35*	*36–45*	*46–55*	*over 55*	*unknown*
1972	North	23.8	41.6	14.7	9.9	5.8	2.0	2.2
	Northeast	26.3	42.9	13.5	8.4	4.5	1.6	2.5
	Southeast	10.3	39.4	19.7	14.9	9.8	3.8	1.6
	South	10.5	45.4	18.0	12.6	7.6	2.9	2.0
	Center-West	16.5	35.4	20.6	13.8	8.3	3.4	3.0
1973	North	15.2	35.7	20.8	16.4	8.1	3.7	0.1
	Northeast	24.7	40.9	14.4	8.8	4.8	2.7	3.7
	Southeast	8.3	43.9	19.5	15.1	8.1	3.9	1.2
	South	8.5	49.1	16.4	11.3	5.1	2.2	7.4
	Center-West	16.4	37.8	18.1	12.4	6.1	3.0	6.2
1972/73	Brazil	18.3	42.2	16.3	11.1	6.1	2.8	3.2

Source: *Relatório da Comissão Parlamentar de Inquérito* (CPI—MOBRAL) *Diário do Congresso Nacional,* 11 May 1976 p. 2332

MOBRAL coordinators claim that these youngsters simply could not be turned away, particularly in areas where there were no schools—such as, to name just one, most of the north of Minas Gerais. 'Students less than fifteen years old usually come with their parents. If we were to send the youngsters away we would lose the trust of the adults who would then also leave the course and remain illiterate.' From 1970 to 1973, more than five million Brazilians became literate, among them 958,996 youngsters between nine and fourteen (see table 26).

MEC statistics show that in 1975 about 4.2 million youngsters between seven and fourteen still had no schools to go to. It is further estimated that about 500,000 youngsters a year drop out of the early grades, to turn into future adult illiterates. In 1975 the backlog of schoolage drop-outs totalled more than two million. These marginals between nine and fourteen—or, as MOBRAL's project called them, *excedentes*—were to be rehabilitated, and then reintegrated into the third year of regular first-level school.

TABLE 26

LITERACY SUCCESS RATE BY AGE GROUPS—1970–73

Region	*9–14*	*15–25*	*26–35*	*36–45*	*46–55*	*over 55*	*unknown*
North	31,992	68,308	35,242	26,930	13,760	5,975	1,180
Northeast	711,307	1,173,042	401,172	246,267	135,937	68,352	95,934
Southeast	121,359	579,352	265,110	204,037	115,832	52,527	17,683
South	57,331	305,047	106,569	73,755	36,445	15,097	39,468
Center-West	36,997	83,873	42,233	28,750	15,029	6,992	11,500
Brazil	958,996	2,200,485	850,326	579,789	317,003	148,943	165,721

Source: *Relatório da Comissão Parlamentar de Inquérito* (CPI—MOBRAL) *Diário do Congresso Nacional,* 11 May 1976, p. 2331.

MOBRAL Infanto-Juvenil's second root was an experimental program which started in Rio Grande do Sul in 1972. Most of its initial 260 students were children of about eleven, from poor families in Porto Alegre. Many of them had already had some schooling but either dropped out of classes or, after repeating the same year over and over again, found adjusting to a new class and to younger classmates impossible. They were given five months of literacy classes, followed by four months of 'integration' classes, and were then returned to school.

The youngsters were taught with a method adapted from that of adult literacy classes, with keywords and concepts changed to suit the world of nine-year old children. Material for the 'integration' classes was culled from MOBRAL's *educação integrada* and combined with parts out of regular school books. The dropout rate was

26 percent, and 70 percent passed their tests to enter third grade. The others were put into second grade.

The experiment was repeated in 1973 in five northeastern states with even greater rates of success which, compared with regional failure rates in regular schools, seemed close to miraculous.

Among the many reasons adduced to abort MOBRAL's project to expand its juvenile 'recuperation' program nationwide, three seem to have been paramount. The first was a protest in Congress that, if one admitted MOBRAL's 'invasion' of the seven to fourteen age group one would also admit 'the failure of basic education in Brazil.' The second was that if MOBRAL were to succeed (and it was fully expected that it would) in reintegrating children into regular school, about one million youngsters a year would reenter public schools totally unable to absorb them. The third reason was the fear that once municipalities were allowed to send their 'excess' children to MOBRAL classes they would stop investing in regular education. The merely transitional project foreseen as a stop-gap would, fatally, become permanent.

Other than that, MOBRAL seems to have survived unscathed. In June 1976 it started testing a new community health-education program in three northeastern states, to be expanded to other states as of 1977. At the same time, the Education Minister announced that, in all likelihood, MOBRAL's activities would continue beyond 1980 (the date when, it is hoped, adult illiteracy in Brazil will have fallen below 10 percent), to concentrate on its community programs. Its next program, tested as usual in one state (Santa Catarina) with the cooperation of the state agricultural federation, will be a sixty-hour course in animal husbandry and planting. MOBRAL's budget for 1977 was US$50 million.

8

Conclusion

WHILE Brazil's education reform laws are being implemented slowly, and often piecemeal, their rationale is being criticized insistently by groups of 'concerned' educators. Both laws are usually being attacked by Brazilian traditionalists as having been 'politically motivated' while being 'alien to Brazilian reality.' What is Brazilian 'reality' as it relates to its educational system?

At the time of the Law of Directives and Bases (1961), Brazilian education was expanding at all three levels, but at rates still far from sufficient to provide for that 'universality' of schooling constitutionally decreed at the primary level, or to provide a satisfactory number of freshman places in higher education. As previously discussed, the share of tax revenues to be applied to education is today a subject of continuing controversy among Brazilian educators, politicians, and technocrats. But there can be no doubt that before the overhaul of the entire tax system in 1967, and the start of the 'economic miracle,' Brazil's social and economic situation was unable to provide a tax base which would have supported universal education. On the other hand, whatever 'options' the educational system offered at the middle-school level, a largely traditional society preferred to cling to the rigidly academic model of the university-oriented French *lycée*. Thus, operating with outdated curricula featuring little more than rote retention of facts, and periodic tests aimed at regurgitating these facts in their prescribed sequence, the education system functioned not as a series of plateaus on the road to graduation, let alone to the labor market, but as a set of filters restraining all but a trickle of the best prepared and most persistent.

The 1964 military revolution did not change Brazilian education or, for that matter, Brazilian society. What the revolution, and the technocrats who came to run the ministries, *did* change was the government's *approach* to education, an approach whose origin in fact went back three decades, to the Vargas years. Education lost its chiefly cultural dimension so beloved by most educators and, instead, came to be seen as the preponderant agent for social and economic change, with, initially, clear stress on the latter. Distressing as it might be from a cultural point of view to have a nation with millions of adult illiterates, and additional millions of marginally schooled, semiliterate children, it was catastrophic from the point of view of national development to lack qualified manpower or, more precisely, 'human capital.'

An illiterate might make an acceptable fisherman, or stonemason, but industrializing Brazil was woefully short of workers sufficiently trained, or trainable, to work in industry. At the upper level, there was an accelerating demand for engineers, scientists, architects, administrators and what is commonly known as 'executives' of all kinds, equipped with the best available training.

THE THRUST OF EDUCATIONAL REFORM

The government's reform efforts have focused largely on formal schooling, from the elementary level through university. Throughout, economic and political considerations have loomed large.

In the mid-sixties, truly first-rate education was available at only three or four Brazilian universities. But higher education's generalized inadequacy, in both numbers and kind, affected Brazil's most vocal sector—its student youth, with whom the military government had been on a collision course since 1964.

In hallowed Latin-American tradition, student groups had been active, and often activist, throughout Brazil's history. Whenever their demands overstepped the bounds of 'genuine' student concerns, their often vociferous claims were either hailed as conducive to progress—or else suppressed. University student groups had been closely allied with the Goulart régime. After the 1964 revolution their leaders were considered too leftist, too inflammatory and, in short, an obstreperous and potentially dangerous element. The military government first sharply curtailed and, after a series of disorders and mass demonstrations in 1967 and 1968, in the end totally suppressed the university students' political activities. However, the government also set out to attempt to remedy at least the legitimate part of their grievances: to improve and expand higher education. Consequently, educational 'reform' legislation (or, as some see it, the foreseeable and inevitable complementation of the 1961 Law) was first enacted at the university level, in 1968, *preceding* that at the basic level by three years.

Even though prominent Brazilian educators had for a number of years deliberated, debated, and refined university reform legislation, and then again postponed it for further elaboration, the promulgation of the University Reform Law in 1968 was unequivocally a 'political' decision. Its implementation was initially tied to economic considerations: Brazil's I. National Development Plan (1971–1974) earmarked special funds for expansion of study places in the 'priority areas' of technical and biomedical sciences (which, in the II. National Development Plan, 1975–1979, also includes agricultural sciences).

A more socially oriented rationale led to the radical innovations of the 1971 Basic Education Law. As Education Minister Jarbas Passarinho put it in early 1971: 'At the end of adolescence, all youngsters are entitled to be qualified to enter the labor force, independent of their possible intention to go on to higher education, and independent of their ability or motivation to do so.' The implied, if never officially admitted, hope was that an adequate education, both academic and practical, would deflect growing numbers of youngsters from unrealistic aspirations to higher education.

One of the concomitant, openly sought after, goals was to redress the imbalance in professional patterns: whereas in the so-called 'priority areas' university graduates were in short supply, middle-level professionals were practically nonexistent. A manpower study made in São Paulo in 1971, for example, showed that there were five engineers for every mechanic, and two doctors for every trained nurse.

Attempts to offer practical education to fill manpower needs for industrial expansion go back to the Vargas years, as already said, but for nearly three decades these offers remained 'options' and could thus be disdained, for questions of social 'status', wherever possible. At the end of the sixties Brazil's accelerating development, and its by then pressing need for trained manpower, triggered the thrust towards innovation in education: the 1971 Law transforms the former options into components of every student's prescribed curriculum.

With all this, Brazil is the only major non-socialist developing nation whose Basic Education Law today prescribes some type of practical training for *all*. Once the 1971 Law is fully implemented children from urban as well as rural families—children of judges, lawyers, doctors, shopkeepers, white-collar workers, blue-collar workers, farmers, carpenters, fishermen—will have to spend some of their time in school with practical, and often even manual, work traditionally frowned upon by Luso-Brazilian culture. For centuries the *anel de bacharel*—the class ring of the baccalaureate and, mostly, the law degree—was the hallmark of the sons from Brazil's upper classes, a status symbol speedily adopted after World War I by Brazil's rising urban middle class. Manual work was for 'the others' and could always be done by the seemingly inexhaustible legions of unschooled and untrained menials who stream to Brazilian cities from the interior.

The Law's intent, aside from its social, developmental and, last but far from least, educational aspects, can thus also be seen as 'egalitarian.' As some claim, this intent is being imposed today on a still predominantly elitist and paternalistic society not at all prepared to admit egalitarian principles, in school or elsewhere.

There is, thus, the question whether, in Brazil, a law such as this will ever be fully implemented. A possible second question is whether it should be.

Quite obviously, any attempt to answer these questions would lead to little but sophistry. In 1976, the University Reform Law was eight years old, and the Basic Education Law five. It might be a bit premature, as well as idle, to look into a crystal ball to try and project the Laws' possible effects twenty years hence, particularly since their implementation (assuming it continues as it has done so far) will inevitably interact with changing social, economic, and political conditions.

Moreover, and in part because of their link with all these extra-educational factors, one can safely expect that both laws will go through some 'adjustments' in the course of their incremental implementation. An astute commentator has said that Brazil is the country of 'experimental laws.' A law is elaborated, and enacted. In spite—or, perhaps, because—of Brazil's monolithic bureaucracies, there is often no way of really enforcing it. Thus, if the law 'takes,' (i.e., if it isn't being disobeyed too flagrantly, or else entirely ignored) it remains in effect. Otherwise, a new law or decree will in due course supersede it. It is unlikely that anything like this will happen with either education reform law, but a major adjustment has already been made, for example, in the 1971 Law. Admittedly, it was a needed and inevitable adjustment to provide a scheme for reducing the originally foreseen plethora of 'professional' courses to groups of manageable, more flexible 'professionalizing' curricula. The adjustment was made by means of a '*parecer*' (an official 'opinion'), CFE *Parecer* no. 76 of January 1975, *not* a decree or an amendment, but in effect equivalent to both. It is thus not unrealistic to presume that in a similar manner other adjustments will gradually be made in some of the aspects of both laws. But it can be assumed that their intent, and basic thrust, will remain as originally enacted.

Instead of projecting, therefore, it might be more appropriate to look briefly at a few of the salient effects of both laws so far, and start, because of their chronological order, with the University Reform Law.

HIGHER EDUCATION

Admissions system and expansion of study places vs. quality of education Table no. 21 on p. 89 shows the enormous expansion of higher education which, as discussed, has resulted chiefly from the mushrooming of private, often substandard, isolated faculties. Here accusations of 'political motivations' are loudest—and in part justified.

There is, to begin with, the decree of 1971 (based on an article in the University Reform Law) which changes the entire university admissions system, the *exame vestibular*. Up to then, aside from its different manipulative aspects, its original 'eliminatory' method had two converse results: by imposing a passing grade—of, say, 5 out of a total score of 8—the system effectively eliminated any candidate who scored below 5, but then also gave anyone achieving that score, or above, the 'right' to university admission.

Students thus 'entitled' to freshman places with frightening regularity exceeded the places available and, in a term well known and officially feared, became *excedentes*. *Excedentes* went to court to enforce their rights. They often won their cases, and imposed themselves on hapless rectors who in turn went to the MEC for help in the form of additional, extra-budgetary funds. Less successful *excedentes* demonstrated, sometimes accompanied by their parents and usually right in front of the MEC which, until 1969, was still in the very heart of Rio de Janeiro. With the new system of 'classifying' *vestibulares* which, in essence, qualified candidates up to the number of freshman places available, many university candidates might still be left out in the cold, but no one who didn't get in could any longer claim, legally or otherwise, that he had a 'right' to be admitted.

The decree thus achieved its patently political goal yet was fully effective mainly because its other provisions, streamlining admissions requirements to acceptable norms, eliminated many of the justified causes for student discontent.

For the students, the new *vestibulares* are still difficult, and in some desirable study areas, such as biomedical sciences, still have about six candidates compete for every available place, but the system is generally considered fair. By doing away with minimum passing grades, the admissions system has indeed become responsive to the candidates' level of instruction—or, as many educators today claim, their level of ignorance.

After each of the *vestibulares unificados*, in Rio de Janeiro, São Paulo, or any of the other 'unified' testing regions, detailed test results are being published in the press. They are invariably accompanied by someone's comment that if a minimum passing grade were required as it formerly was, only a fraction of the now successful candidates would have passed. For traditional professors, the 'classifying' *vestibulares* combined with the 'massification' of study places have created a crisis by dangerously 'lowering the quality' of Brazilian education.

A more balanced view expressed by a handful of experts is that the 'drop' in educational level—in higher education as well as in second-level school—is simply a consequence of social changes and, for the time being, inevitable. More schooling is being made available to larger segments of the population than ever before. It is impossible for the new contingents of students to conform to the patterns of 'presumed excellence' of schools in previous decades with their highly selected clienteles. New educational patterns, to which the yardstick of 'better' or 'worse' simply does not apply, will have to evolve to suit the needs of the new clienteles.

In classical Brazilian contexts, this kind of view is utopian. It is today being voiced openly and publicized, but those who share it will no doubt remain an enlightened minority for a long time to come. The 'back to basics' trend in U.S. classrooms, to fight against near-illiteracy among high school students there, has been watched with empathy, not to say envy, by Brazilian traditionalists for whom a demanding, strictly structured, and rigidly fulfilled academic curriculum remains the only possible panacea for Brazil's scholastic woes.

Foreseeably, the new fairness of Brazilian *vestibulares* will once more be tempered with more exacting scholastic requirements.

UNIVERSITY AUTONOMY AND STUDENT POLITICS

The universities' chief grievance against the new admissions system has been that it infringed on their 'autonomy.' They could no longer control, and determine without anyone's interference, the type of candidates they would admit. This may in part be true from a purely academic perspective, although the different universities have been found to cope satisfactorily with that aspect, too. Even though higher education's 'basic cycle' still does not function the way it should, it is expected to help students make up for inadequate second-level instruction; the ones who don't can be expelled. (The number of expulsions, after repeated failures, is small.) Others may drop out, as they have always done, for a variety of reasons.

Students continue to protest the universities' expulsion procedures as being unfair to those who are both studying and working to support themselves (about 50 percent of all Brazilian university students). Most of them claim that, since they are in fact studying part-time, they are simply unable to complete course requirements successfully, without repeated initial failures. Still, student protests about 'unfairness' within the universities are less frequent and those that occur are usually kept at lower decibels than would have been the case before 1969. Student activities in the universities are being controlled by the innovations of the University Reform Law.

The Law has two stipulations for student representation: (1) that one-fifth of the members of university governing bodies shall be constituted by elected student representatives, with both voice and vote; (2) that students 'may' congregate in organizations (usually, *diretórios acadêmicos*, or DAs at the faculty level, headed by the *Diretório Central dos Estudantes*, DCE, at the university level) and elect their officers. But these officers are not 'representative,' i.e., they are *a priori excluded* from representing their constituents in the university governing bodies, instead of being automatically part of them, as in the past. Also, adding insult to injury, only students with satisfactory academic records can be eligible as 'student representatives.'

With this division, the formerly essential student organizations became irrelevant and thus, for many rectors, expendable. In Rio de Janeiro, for example, most of the existing DAs and DCEs had been dissolved or suspended in 1968 and early 1969. They remained closed, pending the adoption of new university charters, or charter revisions. At the University of Brasília (UnB), the first elections for student organizations were slated to be held in May 1976, six years after UnB's new charter made these elections possible and, in fact, necessary. The election campaign allegedly turned 'subversive' through the distribution of pamphlets dealing with such nonstudent concerns as the state of national politics, the Institutional Act 5, and decree-law 477. Election preparations were stopped, seven students were expelled, and twelve students were suspended.

Decree-law 477 of February 1969 curbs political activities in the universities by students as well as professors; it provides for the expulsion of students, professors, and staff for disciplinary infractions of a 'subversive' nature. This covers a multitude of serious crimes as well as of innocuous misdemeanors, plus the 'intent' to commit them. Anyone found guilty by university authorities of any of these infractions can be expelled and, if he is a student, *prevented from rematriculating at any Brazilian university for 3 years.* If the culprit is a professor or administrator, he cannot be reemployed at any university for a period of 5 years.

Altogether, decree-law 477 has been applied against 215 persons in 1969 (all but five of them students) and 38 in the following four years. Since then, decree-law 477 seems to have fallen into disuse but, as students and politicians point out, its *possible* use continues to hang over university communities like a Damocles sword. Most of the damage, needless to say, has been done precisely by the decree's mere existence and its availability as a threat against any dissenter in university communities. Many politicians have for years deplored the existence of decree-law 477 and advocated its abolition.

In fact, decree-law 477 filled most of the purpose for which it was intended, right or wrong, within the first nine months of its existence. Moreover, the final decision over the use of 477 was, in each case, brought under the jurisdiction of the MEC in 1972. Thereafter its application was no longer 'autonomous' and thus rapidly lost its attractiveness for the individual rector. On the other hand, most rectors have and always had adequate provisions right in their charters for coping with 'subversion' so far as their own universities are concerned, as the 1976 expulsions at UnB have clearly shown. Except that without resorting to decree-law 477 a rector cannot prevent anyone he may expel from at least trying to gain readmission elsewhere. That facet of decree-law 477 has long since lost its expediency, as has the rest of the decree. But its threat survives, as an exacerbating symbol of political constraints in Brazilian universities.

Moreover, decree-law 477 retains its function as an insidious academic curb. Communism, marxism, and all types and shadings of leftist ideology became taboo in Brazil after 1964. Having been purged of their marxist professors, some of them scientists of world renown, Brazilian universities may in the eyes of the military government have lost much of their dangerous proclivity for ideological contamination. However, the stringent ideological restrictions imposed upon open debate among students and professors in some areas—particularly economics, the social sciences, and the humanities—have turned into critical academic liabilities.

With all its dynamic industrial and economic development, Brazil is today still part of the Third World. As it happens, the study of Third World problems has so far been tackled chiefly, and with often notable results, by famous scientists with marxist convictions such as the respected pre-Pinochet Chilean social scientists and economists, and the internationally famous French leftist intellectuals. By precluding the inquiry into research made by marxist intellectuals because, or so it is presumed, such inquiry must automatically lead to the advocacy of marxist solutions for Brazilian problems, the enforced ideological bias prevailing at Brazilian universities is engendering intellectual blind spots among their students.

EXCESSIVE EXPANSION OF HIGHER EDUCATION

The trend most deplored by conservative educators is the ballooning of student numbers in recent years, and particularly the fact that available freshman places practically doubled between 1970 and 1975 (see table 21, p. 89). The magic word here is 'available.' Already in 1973, supply exceeded demand by 32,000 places. In 1974, 76,598 available freshman places remained unfilled, and in 1975 *São Paulo alone* had 70,000 freshman places which remained unfilled. The hardest hit are inevitably the private faculties which overestimated the demand for their often unattractive facilities and simply overexpanded. Thus, while the demand for places in public universities, with their controlled educational standards but limited rates of growth, will remain high, the overall expansion of higher education seems to have levelled off to manageable proportions.

QUALIFICATION AND STATUS OF PROFESSORS

While professors protest the inadequate preparation of students admitted to higher education, many university rectors tend to agree that the chief culprit for the drop in the quality of instruction is their teaching staff which, they claim, consists largely of professors without pedagogic experience or the cultural background necessary to teach at a university. The rectors' complaint is partly justified; the flaw they criticize is in fact rooted in the relative youth and the improvised expansion of Brazilian higher education, and the type of professors available for it. The old traditional faculties, of law and medicine, for example, had the best professionals in their field as professors. They taught part-time, to be sure, but their intellectual and cultural prominence, and their acknowledged professional and social status, made them eminently qualified to lecture to students—for that is in essence all that they did. In recent decades, the masses of professors needed for Brazil's massifying higher education were largely culled from those staffing the *colégios*, the upper middle-level schools. These *colégio* professors, of widely varying proficiency, then proceeded to do in the faculties exactly what they had done in the *colégios*: they *taught* their students—facts, data, and lessons in strictly circumscribed subject matters—instead of stimulating research and motivating the students to investigate and learn on their own.

Another and more recent cause of the shortage of qualified university professors is a kind of brain-drain from the universities to the labor market, as one of the side-effects of Brazil's economic boom. Today's salary scales for professors at public universities, for full-time or part-time teaching, may seem adequate if compared with those of other qualified public employees. The same professors, however, if they are trained in one of the professions at present in short supply—engineering, administration, nutrition, surgery, to name just a few—can earn at least four times the salaries they get for teaching at a public university. Even first-rate private universities cannot, as a rule, compete with the salaries offered by Brazilian industries today for qualified professionals. But, on the other hand, some prestigious private universities, and a few public universities such as the State University of São Paulo and the State University of Campinas, can offer their professors excellent teaching and research facilities which are unavailable at other Brazilian universities, and thus make up for salary discrepancies.

The apparent lack of interest in teaching as a career is further confirmed by the fact that many of the freshman places which recently remained unfilled were in *faculdades de filosofia*, teachers' colleges and other branches of higher education leading specifically to teaching careers in universities and second-level schools.

At regular intervals suggestions are voiced that, unless Brazil wants to resign itself to having only second-raters teach at its universities, professors should be shown 'the esteem due them' which, inevitably, means that they should be better paid than they are now. On the other hand, it would be impossible, as was recently pointed out by an academic dean, for the federal government to pay salaries on the order of US$4,000 a month to each one of the professors teaching full-time at federal universities merely to prevent their exodus to other jobs. An interim solution seems to be, once more, a reversion to part-time teaching so as to keep first-rate professionals teaching at all.

BASIC EDUCATION LAW

Faltering implementation of professionalizing second-level education The 1971 Basic Education Law is notable for two innovations. The first and more visible one is the institution of vocational and professional training cycles—inconvenient, expensive, and with general benefits still largely unknown.

Educators who favor the professionalizing cycle in second-level school are, needless to say, far less vocal than the ones who oppose it. The opponents say that the second-level school, the former *colégio*, has traditionally served to train Brazil's elites. Youngsters who had successfully run the gamut of the lower grades went through the upper grades aiming infallibly towards higher education, and felt fully justified in doing so. This is a goal which is not about to change, they claim. But while higher education was streamlined and expanded after 1968, the 1971 Basic Education Law, conversely, weakens the already tenuous preparation of university candidates: three years of class hours, where academic disciplines must cover the same ground as before but are now reduced by the share they must relinquish to professionalizing courses, are once more inadequate to prepare students for higher education.

A far more balanced assessment was made by the President of the Rio de Janeiro State Education Council, who said that second-level school was entirely new, with other goals, other objectives, and other implications. It is evident that the second-level school will be hard pressed to offer its students more than elitist, university-oriented instruction once first-level schools admit, retain, and graduate the masses of youngsters entitled to basic education.

But still, one might ask why even future contingents of Brazilian second-level school students should decide to content themselves with the 'terminality' of professionalizing education. The question is analyzed and, incidentally, answered with tempered pessimism, by Cláudio de Moura Castro, in a study called 'Professionalizing Second-Level School: The Consolation Prize?' ('Secundário Profissionalizante: Prêmio de Consolação?') This study is worth examining in some detail since it deals, in closely reasoned arguments, with the full gamut of factors bearing on the implementation of Brazil's new second-level schooling.

In essence, the study argues that so long as a university degree in Brazil continues to offer vastly higher economic and social rewards than a second-level school degree, professionalizing or not, the overwhelming majority of second-level school graduates, whatever their numbers, will continue to aim, single-mindedly, towards higher education. Since for obvious reasons Brazil's higher education can satisfy no more than part of that demand, the majority of second-level school graduates will find themselves frustrated. And, instead of valuing their degree as a worthwhile culmination of eleven years of schooling, they will see it as little more than a 'consolation prize'—and, further, a prize of decreasing value if present trends continue.

In the last few years, Brazilian second-level school graduates have found it more and more difficult to enter the labor market. Many of the jobs formerly filled by them are being taken up by university graduates. It is in fact not at all surprising that Brazilian employers should disdain to hire second-level school graduates and prefer hiring university graduates, who have in recent years graduated in ever-increasing numbers (see table 17). In a classical market economy, these ever-increasing numbers should eventually glut labor markets and, in an inevitable sequence, leave more and more university graduates unemployed, depress salary scales for those who can find jobs, and ultimately reduce the economic value of a university degree and thus invalidate the chief incentive for many of those today pressuring for higher education. But in Brazil that market economy mechanism has been tampered with, and in effect neutralized, through government regulations enacted in part under pressure from professional associations.

Anyone who graduates from a Brazilian university and is therefore entitled to professional status must register his diploma with the appropriate professional association. Without that registration he cannot legally be employed as a professional. The type and amount of training required for every profession is regulated by the government through the different Education Councils. But in addition, there are different kinds of professional occupations—in banks, in corporations, in government offices—for which a university degree is prescribed.

The number and range of these officially circumscribed occupations have widened in recent years. One reason for that is simply that university graduates with the most varied professional qualifications are available today, whereas they were in short supply before, when some sectors of the nation's expanding economy, unable to find the desired university graduates, had to make do instead with graduates from second-level schools—or, as they were then still called, *colégios*.

Another, more insidious reason for the growth in the number of occupations being officially declared off-limits for anyone not endowed with the proper professional certificates is what the study calls 'a rebirth of medieval corporatism.' Concerned with ensuring employment opportunities for the new legions of credentialled job-seekers, Brazil's clannish professional associations are pressuring the government to set aside a widening variety of occupations as the exclusive domain of university graduates, whose employment then should become compulsory for public enterprises as well as public bureaucracies.

Consequently, while a growing variety of employment opportunities is made available to Brazilian university graduates, the second-level school graduates see themselves deprived by government fiat, so to speak, of a number of employment chances formerly available to them and traditionally filled satisfactorily by them.

The economic value of a second-level school degree is thus diminished. But this, in turn, also reflects on the private cost of higher education. A Brazilian second-level school student, when figuring out the price he will have to pay for going on to higher education, includes in his calculations the earnings he must forgo while he continues his studies. If he figures that by continuing his education he would deprive himself of a desirable, full-time job with a good salary, he might find the cost of higher education high, perhaps too high. But what if his chances for finding a job are doubtful? Or if he can only find a poorly paying job? Then he will lose little by going on to get that coveted university degree which, in turn, will seem so much more precious and desirable.

Fully acknowledging the intrinsic value, in Brazilian contexts, of professionalizing second-level education, the study ends with three conclusions. The first one is that wherever second-level classes include children from working-class backgrounds as well as those from middle-class families, the forces of social dynamics will make the former adopt—eagerly, automatically, and nearly inevitably—the social values of the latter, including their traditional prejudices against manual occupations.

The second conclusion is that the great expense of efficient professionalizing training can so far be borne only by Brazil's prestigious private schools. But in these private schools it is essentially wasted on their inevitably university-bound clientele (see p. 77). But public second-level schools, with students from modest social backgrounds and with a genuine need for—and potential appreciation of—professionalizing education, are unable to shoulder the expense of such training unless they are assisted, at least initially, by massive financial support from the government.

And, thirdly, the study concludes that by now (early 1976) the government must have become aware that its purported and amply propagated objective—of wanting to deflect the assault on Brazilian universities by making professionalizing second-level education possible, and acceptable, to growing numbers of Brazilian youngsters—is in fact being sabotaged by contradictory strategies.

The successful implementation of professionalizing education in Brazil, consequently, remains subject to stripping university education of its insiduous props, and to infusing massive funds into public second-level schools.

SCHOLASTIC PERFORMANCE AND VOCATIONAL TRAINING IN FIRST-LEVEL SCHOOLS

The Law's second notable innovation is the attempt to ease Brazilian children's year-end trauma by stipulating that for year-end promotion 'the results obtained during the academic year shall have greater weight than those of the year-end examinations.' It is obvious that children who get promoted are less likely to drop out of school. At the same time, a smaller rate of repeaters in first and second grades will make more places available for new entrants.

Added to these purely pedagogic considerations is the awareness that young children from poor families simply can not be expected to conform, initially, to *any* set academic standards and that they may have to be kept in school and promoted *in spite of* their poor scholastic performance. To quote a statement made by the Education Secretary in Rio de Janeiro in July 1976: 'If the child does not become literate the first year, but succeeds in socializing and taking an interest in its community, it is important that this child should be promoted so that it doesn't drop out. It [the child] can become literate the next year.' (*Jornal do Brasil*, 21 July 1976.)

Children with inadequate grades should, according to the Law, go into 'recuperation classes' during school vacations. In São Paulo, for example, 130,000 municipal school students went into remedial classes during July 1976. (This, it should be noted, was a first for São Paulo's municipal schools, fully five years after the Law decreed it.) An extra allocation of funds was needed to pay for the 7,000 teachers working in the program, but it was hoped that these classes would pay for themselves by reducing São Paulo's high rate of first-grade repeaters which until 1976 had oscillated between 45 and 72 percent.

The vocational cycle in first-level school is often being referred to as the 'Americanization' of Brazilian education. There is no question that the Ford Foundation, for one, has been instrumental in helping to revamp, streamline, and otherwise rationalize teacher training programs at *faculdades de filosofia* in selected southern universities, to make the process of teacher qualifications less cumbersome, and more versatile. The models for these processes, however, were elaborated by Brazilian educators and projected to fit a 'reformed' basic education.

A far more visible—and far more controversial—role was played by the U.S. Agency for International Development with its US$64 million loan agreement of 1969, matched by Brazilian funds, to help finance the projection, building, and equipping of nearly 300 model schools all over Brazil, and the training of teachers and administrators to staff them. The schools were *ginásios orientados para o trabalho*, or GOTs, as they were then known, the 'work-oriented' lower middle-level schools which, with the 1971 Law, became grades five through eight of first-level education. The idea of combining general studies with vocational training at that level was conceived by Anísio Teixeira, one of Brazil's most renowned and progressive educators; a number of GOTs had already been organized in different Brazilian states in the early sixties. It was Teixeira's concept, and not something dreamed up by USAID, which was incorporated into the 1971 Basic Education Law.

The model GOTs are large school units, each one fully and properly equipped with 'shops' which have been criticized because, as constructed, they are suitable only for Brazil's urban areas. But the 1971 Law prescribes systems and not edifices, and already foresees 'inter-school centers' as a more flexible, and far cheaper, system of 'shops' for vocational training.

Critics of the Law have repeatedly pointed out that it does not make sense to prescribe vocational training in grades five through eight while schools in Brazil's rural areas, so far as they exist at all, often do not go beyond first grade. The MEC has repeatedly stated that by 1979 at least the first four grades of public first-level schools will be available to *all* Brazilian children. Yet no one should underestimate the enormous difficulties in bringing this about.

There is, first of all, the stark fact that social and economic change must *precede* the construction of schools if anyone wants education to take a hold in Brazil's rural hinterlands. Most of Brazil's rural areas, and particularly those in the Center-West and the Northeast, are so far unable to retain a stable population of rural families. The absence of an effective agrarian reform, coupled with archaic and inefficient agricultural production methods, continue to prevent rural workers from settling in one place for more than two or three years, and this precludes any semblance of systematic schooling for their children.

The more dramatic aspect of the same problem is Brazil's sustained urbanization rate. Between 1960 and 1975 the proportion of Brazilians living in urban areas rose from 46.2 to 63.5 percent. This means, in absolute numbers, that 33 million people, out of a national total of close to 71 million, had swelled to 69 million fifteen years later when Brazil's population totalled 108 million.

Occasional statements by educational officials that under these conditions attempts to expand rural education are bound to remain ineffectual can thus be understood. Yet, since Brazilian society unequivocally continues to prefer formal over nonformal education, it must as a consequence also make schools available for children in the hinterlands. The price for that may have to be a greater federal participation in the funding of first-level education.

While the federal government tries to increase its share of education funding through extrabudgetary allocations, critics insist that funding of that type is far too susceptible to fluctuations in Brazil's economy, and that the only way to provide safe and reliable education funding is to set aside a fixed yearly share of the federal budget. Thus, the aborted project in Congress to make a 12 percent yearly share compulsory.

The role of educational investment In the last five years, some of Brazil's most renowned economists have analyzed the different aspects of education as they relate to Brazil's development. Their studies bear out the need for increased investments in education, as well as their profitability.

The Graduate School of Economics of the Fundação Getúlio Vargas has shown in one of its recent analyses that education in the form of a better trained and thus more productive labor force has been responsible for a 1 percent yearly growth in Brazil's GDP between 1960 and 1970. The Fundação's study has further shown that in 1969 the average return for investments in education was around 28 percent, and thus nearly *twice* that obtained with capital investments (machinery, equipment, construction), which was about 14 percent. The conclusion reached by the Fundação's economists was, therefore, that far too little money was being invested in Brazilian education and that economic growth could be accelerated merely by transferring a slice of the funds applied to capital accumulation towards a faster accumulation of human capital.

Furthermore, and considering the proven link between the Brazilians' level of education and level of income, the economists suggest that government efforts to make better education available to greater numbers of people are important not only to maintain Brazil's economic growth, but also to raise the income levels of wider population segments and thus to achieve a wider distribution of the fruits of that growth.

Economic analyses have further supported the importance of universal basic education. In comparing the returns of investments at the different educational levels, the figures show that completed higher education gives the highest *private* return, but that the highest *social* return results from investments in basic education.

Even though traditional educators with their concern for cultural values persistently criticize the government for its stress of education as an agent for economic development, there is no question that findings such as these are paramount to accelerating educational expansion in Brazil—as well as, in the process, accelerating the cultural impact of education on growing numbers of Brazilians of all ages.

ENSINO SUPLETIVO

The 1971 Basic Education Law has for the first time created a 'system' of nonformal education. The components of that system, as shown in chapter seven, range from the most varied type of instruction preparing for equivalency exams to a variety of workers' training courses; they are also producing the most varied results.

Hardly any comment is necessary regarding SENAI, SENAC, and other manpower training programs. They are urgently needed. After decades of being widely disdained as being merely 'salvage programs' for unschooled youngsters from poor families, professional training programs have become respected, and sought after. They, too, now lead to economic and social mobility.

A little less clearcut, at least so far, are the results of some of the other, essentially 'equivalent education,' programs. It is difficult to evaluate the efficiency of the educational radio and television programs. Rio de Janeiro's educational television serial, 'João da Silva,' boasted of the 43 percent approval rate of its students in 1974, but the total number of students who presented themselves for exams was about 1,500 out of more than 12,000 who had reportedly taken part in the program. This can hardly be considered a representative sample if one considers the size of the audience reached by a television program broadcast in Rio de Janeiro during prime time.

There are no official figures available concerning the 2,675,161 candidates who sat for *exames supletivos* nationwide in 1975, to show how many had studied in '*cursinhos*' or prepared themselves through radio or television instruction or other means. Since the contents and standards of the tests also still vary from state to state, the national failure rate of 65.7 percent is indicative of little but the need to improve both the testing mechanisms and the preparation of the candidates.

Opinions about the value of parallel education programs in Brazilian contexts are sharply divided. Progressives see the unprecedented chances given to partially schooled people of all ages to catch up, to improve themselves and perhaps their earning possibilities and, on the whole, to learn whenever and wherever they can. Traditional educators, on the other hand, look askance particularly at the growing number of public and private *cursos supletivos seriados* as being a diluted surrogate for formal education and merely a shortcut to the coveted graduation certificate. The *cursos supletivos seriados*, it must be remembered, may organize their own final exams which, some say, are often far less demanding than the new state *exames supletivos*.

There is no question that Brazilian society continues to cherish formal education and its diplomas and rewards them in the market place. A recent doctoral thesis by a young economist from the Getúlio Vargas Foundation has analyzed the relationship between schooling, job experience, and earnings in Brazil. Among the study's salient findings is that 'an increase of one year in schooling has a substantially larger impact on individual earnings than an increase of one year in job experience,' and that 'the returns to the terminal years of a cycle of education are greater than the returns to the earlier years,' and that this reveals the existence of a 'diploma effect.' (Senna, unpublished dissertation.)

And so one can hardly blame young Brazilians if they look for all possible ways to obtain the coveted graduation certificates. This also explains the desire, lately supported by the necessary testing systems, of successful professional employees with incomplete schooling to have their qualifications officially certified by *exames supletivos professionalizantes*.

One should, of course, not forget the masses of people all over Brazil who may have absorbed, haphazardly, some part of one of the educational courses now offered in profusion on all Brazilian mass media, and who never presented themselves for any tests. If one judges education from a traditional point of view, then these people 'achieved' nothing that can be measured either academically or economically. But for progressives, and for government planners, their intangible achievement is valuable in another area. Countless government programs in Brazil's poorer areas, particularly in the Northeast, are stalled not for lack of funds but because the people whom these programs are supposed to benefit are uneducated, trapped in old-fashioned ways and unable to adapt to new ones. Nonformal education, even partial nonformal education not crowned by any type of diploma, helps to foster a change of attitude indispensable for development. In one word, modernization.

MOBRAL

This 'change of attitude' may also be one of the chief achievements of MOBRAL whose success in making people literate, once and for all, will forever remain questionable to traditionalists. Nor is that 'once-and-for-all' literacy possible in rural areas. Literacy, if already they achieve it in MOBRAL's five-months' courses, is of little use to rural workers on Bahia's cocoa plantations, for example, even though their living conditions are as a rule far better than those of workers on northeastern sugar plantations. What MOBRAL may do for the cocoa workers is to make them want to take, subsequently, one of the intensive two- or three-week agricultural training courses offered by different organizations in the cocoa region, and thus increase their efficiency and earnings.

Looking at MOBRAL as a whole, it has very much the 'boomerang effect' which developing nations have found so hard to cope with. Young people under twenty-five who have achieved some modicum of education at a low level invariably press for more instruction at the next-higher one. Adults, once they become literate, also become far more conscious of the need of education for their children. A survey made in 1975 in Rio Grande do Sul found that 37.2 percent of workers who had had less than four years of basic education (i.e., incomplete primary, in former terms) wanted their children to go through higher education. The aspirations of workers who went to MOBRAL were not only, as expected, much higher than those of workers who had never gone to school at all, but also higher than the aspirations of the workers with incomplete primary schooling. In MOBRAL 74.7 percent of workers said that they wanted their children to go to a university. Further research showed that workers going to MOBRAL classes had a more definite vision of the importance and the need of an advanced formal education for their children.

Adult literacy movements have a clear 'motivation' component so as to stimulate individuals beyond school age to want and to accept instruction. The most famous method of making adults literate is the Paulo Freire method; it aims to make people literate in six weeks and has *concientização* (consciousness raising) as its most effective component. Aside from the fact that *concientização* is part of a leftist ideology and thus unacceptable to the Brazilian government, Brazilian planners have argued that it would be unfair to poor people to expose them to short, intensive periods of 'literacy training with consciousness raising' since that would raise their demands beyond any that can be fulfilled, short-term, by any developing nation. MOBRAL's 'socializing' component is clearly one of progress-through-work-within-the-existing-social-structure. And, with equal clarity, MOBRAL seeks to spark the desire for more education which, in Brazilian terms, means more schooling.

It can be expected that some of that demand will be satisfied through MOBRAL's 'parallel education empire', assuming that MOBRAL will be permitted to continue its work. Another part will, without a doubt, have to be shouldered by the regular school system. Aside from the argument that MOBRAL's program to make school-age children literate was 'unconstitutional,' as well as the one that a 'temporary' children's literacy program might well turn permanent, the fact remains that, in practice, MOBRAL's *Programa Infanto Juvenil* had to be aborted also because the school system would have been unable to absorb millions of newly literate children. If nothing else, this phase of MOBRAL showed once more to anyone who still needed to be convinced that Brazil's basic school system must be expanded and made more productive, and that sufficient funds—and efforts—must be applied to that task.

It is quite evident that Brazil's education reform is progressing slowly and under a series of stresses which, particularly in basic education, are inextricably linked with extra-educational factors. The unsettled lives of rural workers' families in Brazil's vast interior make the systematic schooling of their children nearly impossible. On the other hand, Brazil's sustained urbanization rate brings masses of culturally unprepared children into urban schools. In higher education, educators are concerned with the inevitable, and it is hoped only temporary, drop in academic standards due to rapid massification. Social pressures for college degrees have so far remained practically unchanged.

As Brazil continues to pursue its development goals and strives for world power status, there is every reason to expect that the government will continue—and most likely strengthen—its support for educational change and expansion.

Bibliography

NOTE ON SOURCES AND TERMINOLOGY

We would like to add here a few words regarding the sources we used for this study. Anyone who will, like ourselves, set out to do educational research in Brazil today will appreciate, as we did, the growing number of excellent education studies now being published there, as well as their widening scope. But, as mentioned in our foreword, a researcher may also find that most of these recent studies are highly technical, scholarly and specific, and as a rule are limited to small areas of investigation. On the other hand, all comprehensive education books, written by Brazilian educators or social scientists involved with education, date from before 1971.

Since it seemed essential to us to work with the most recent data available, we had to rely heavily on government material: data presented at periodic regional meetings of public education officials; material made available by the various State Education Secretariats, and publications prepared and distributed by the MEC. Most of this material was couched in totally bland and uncritical language. Another source for latest data was the daily press which, incidentally, provides remarkably ample coverage of education news; here the data were often accompanied by unbalanced criticism, or bolstered by biased and clearly polemical arguments. In trying to strike a fair balance between the two, it is possible that in some parts of this study we may have leaned a bit towards the bland and uncritical.

We would also like to comment briefly on the terminology we used. At the time the Brazilians projected the 1971 Education Reform Law, they already used a varied and slightly confusing sequential terminology: there were *series* (grades), *ciclos* (cycles), and *níveis* (levels). For the 'new' school, the Brazilians kept the *series* for the grades, but divided the structure into *graus* (degrees), to show the difference from the old system. However, we translated the new *escola de 1° grau* and *escola de 2° grau* into 'first-*level*' and 'second-*level*' school, and not into 'first-degree' and 'second-degree' school, as it would have been in a literal translation and as it was initially done in some official documents. (One inevitable result of that translation would be, for example, that Brazilian university would be called 'third-degree school.') Since we were among the first non-Brazilians to write about the new Brazilian education, we easily got Brazilian education authorities to agree to, and in fact prefer, our free translation of their terminology. We hope that our readers, too, will agree with what we did and perhaps follow our example.

BOOKS

Altbach, Philip G., ed. *Turmoil and Transition: Higher Education and Student Politics in India*. New York: Basic Books, 1969

——, and Kelly, Daniel H. *Higher Education in Developing Nations: A Selected Bibliography, 1969–1974*. New York: Praeger Publishers, 1974

de Azevedo, Fernando. *Brazilian Culture*. New York: Macmillan Company, 1950

Baer, Werner. *Industrialization and Economic Development in Brazil*. Homewood, Ill: Irwin, 1965

Baklanoff, Eric N., ed. *The Shaping of Modern Brazil*. Baton Rouge: Louisiana State University Press, 1969

Banks, Arthur S., ed. *Political Handbook of the World: 1975*. New York: McGraw-Hill, 1975

Benjamin, Harold. *Higher Education in the American Republics*. New York: McGraw-Hill, 1965

Blaug, Mark. *Education and the Employment Problem in Developing Countries*. Geneva: International Labour Office, 1973

Coombs, Philip H. *The World Educational Crisis*. New York: Oxford University Press, 1968

da Cunha, Nádia Franco. *Vestibular na Guanabara*. Rio de Janeiro: Ministério da Educação e Cultura, 1968

Daland, Robert T. *Brazilian Planning: Development Politics and Administration*. Chapel Hill: University of North Carolina Press, 1967

Dines, Alberto, ed. *Os Idos de Março e a Queda em Abril*. Rio de Janeiro: José Alvaro Editor, 1964

Dulles, John W. F. *Vargas of Brazil*. Austin: University of Texas Press, 1967

Faure, Edgar et al. *Learning to Be*. Paris: UNESCO, 1972

Fernandes, Florestan. *Educação e Sociedade no Brasil*. São Paulo: Dominus Editôra, 1966

——. *Universidade Brasileira: Reforma ou Revolução*? São Paulo: Editôra Alfa-Omega, 1975

Fiechter, George-André. *Le Régime 'Modernisateur' du Brésil: 1964–1972*. Genève: Institut Universitaire de Hautes Etudes Internationales, 1972

Foracchi, Marialice M. *O Estudante e a Transformacão da Sociedade Brasileira*. São Paulo: Companhia Editora Nacional, 1965

——. *A Juventude na Sociedade Moderna*. São Paulo: Universidade de São Paulo, 1972

Freire, Paulo. *Cultural Action for Freedom*, Monograph Series No. 1. Cambridge, Mass.: Harvard Educational Review and the Center for the Study of Development and Social Change, 1970

Grande, Humberto. *A Pedagogia no Estado Nôvo*. Rio de Janeiro: Gráfica Guarany Ltda., 1941

Haar, Jerry. *The Politics of Higher Education in Brazil*. New York: Praeger Publishers, 1977

Havighurst, Robert J., and Moreira, J. Roberto. *Society and Education in Brazil*. Pittsburgh: University of Pittsburgh Press, 1965

Kogan, Maurice. *The Government of Education*. London: Macmillan, 1971

Lambert, Jacques. *Os Dois Brasís*. Rio de Janeiro: Centro Brasileiro de Pesquisas Educacionais, 1959

Langoni, Carlos Geraldo. *Distribuição da Renda e Desenvolvimento Econômico do Brasil.* Rio de Janeiro: Editôra Expressão e Cultura, 1973

Lauwerys, Joseph A., and Scanlon, David, eds. *The World Year Book of Education, 1969.* New York: Harcourt, Brace and Jovanovich, 1969

Liebman, Arthur; Walker, Kenneth; and Glazer, Myron. *Latin American University Students: A Six Nation Study.* Cambridge, Mass.: Harvard University Press, 1972

Lima, Lauro de Oliveira. *Estorias da Educação no Brasil: de Pombal a Passarinho.* 2a edição. Rio de Janeiro: Editora Brasília, n.d.

McNeill, Malvina Rosat. *Guidelines to Problems of Education in Brazil: A Review and Selected Bibliography.* New York: Teachers College Press, Columbia University, 1970

Moacir, Primitivo. *A Instrução e o Império.* São Paulo: Companhia Editôra Nacional, n.d.

Moreira, J. Roberto. *Educação e Desenvolvimento no Brasil.* Rio de Janeiro: Centro Latino-Americano de Pesquisas em Ciências Sociais, 1960

Paiva, Vanilda Pereira. *Educação Popular e Educação de Adultos: Contribuição e História da Educação Brasileira.* São Paulo: Edições Loyola, 1973

Poerner, Arthur José. *O Poder Jovem.* Rio de Janeiro: Editôra Civilização Brasileira, 1968

Robock, Stefan. *Brazil: A Study in Development Progress.* Lexington, Mass.: D. C. Heath and Co., 1975

Rodrigues, Mauro Costa. *As Reformas do Ensino: Contribuição de um Modêlo de Sistema Educacional.* Rio de Janeiro: Relex, 1975

Rodrigues da Cunha, Luiz Antonio. *A Profissionalização no Ensino Médio.* Rio de Janeiro: Livraria Eldorado Tijuca Ltda., 1974

Rosenbaum, H. Jon, and Tyler, William G., eds. *Contemporary Brazil: Issues in Economic and Political Development.* New York: Praeger Publishers, 1972

Ruddle, K., and Oderman, D., eds. *Statistical Abstract of Latin America, 1971.* Los Angeles: Latin American Center, University of California at Los Angeles, 1972

Schiefelbein, Ernesto and McGinn, Noel F. eds. *Universidad Contemporánea: Intento de Análisis Empírico.* Santiago: Corporación de Promoción Universitária, 1974

Schneider, Ronald M. *The Political System of Brazil: Emergence of a Modernizing Authoritarian Regime, 1964–1970.* New York: Columbia University Press, 1971

Simonsen, Mário Henrique. *Brasil 2002.* Rio de Janeiro: APEC Editora, 1972

Solari, Aldo E., ed. *Estudiantes y Política en América Latina.* Caracas: Monte Avila Editores, 1968

Stepan, Alfred, ed. *Authoritarian Brazil: Origins, Policies, and Future.* New Haven: Yale University Press, 1973

Syvrud, Donald E. *Foundations of Brazilian Economic Growth.* Stanford: Hoover Institution Press, Stanford University, 1974

Tavares de Miranda, Maria do Carmo. *Educação no Brasil.* Recife: Imprensa Universitária, 1966

Teixeira, Anísio. *Educação no Brasil,* 2a edição. São Paulo: Companhia Editora Nacional, 1976

Viana, Oliveira. *Evolução do Povo Brasileiro,* 4a edição. Rio de Janeiro, 1956

Wagley, Charles. *An Introduction to Brazil.* New York: Columbia University Press, 1971

Werebe, Maria José Garcia. *Grandezas e Misérias do Ensino no Brasil.* São Paulo: Difusão Européia do Livro, 1970

ARTICLES AND PERIODICALS

Barcellos, Osvaldo. 'Excedente não desaparece como num passe de mágica.' *Diário de Notícias,* 24 January 1971

Beltrão, Hélio. 'A Revolução da Educação.' *O Cruzeiro,* 23 October 1969

Bowles, Frank. 'Access to Higher Education.' Vol. 1. Liège, Belgium: UNESCO and the International Association of Universities, 1963

Brandão Lopes, J. R. 'Estrutura social e educaçao no Brasil.' *Educacão e Ciências Sociais* 4 (April 1959): 53–77

Cardoso, Fernando Henrique. 'Educação e mudança social.' *Pesquisa e Planejamento* 5 (5): 55–56

Castello Branco, Carlos. 'O emprêgo da técnica.' *Jornal do Brasil*, 19 September 1972

Castro, Cláudio de Moura. 'Investimento em educação no Brasil: uma réplica.' *Pesquisas de Planejamento* 1 (December 1971): 393–401

——. 'Investimento em educação no Brasil: Comparacão de três estudos.' *Pesquisas de Planejamento*, 1 (June/November 1971): 141–152

——. 'Secundário Profissionalizante: Prêmio de Consolação?' *Cadernos de Pesquisa*, Fundação Carlos Chagas, 17 (June 1976): 41–52

Chagas, Valnir. 'A admissão à universidade e a Lei de Diretrizes e Bases.' *Revista Brasileira de Estudos Pedagógicos* 37 (January–March 1962)

——. 'A seleção e o vestibular na reforma universitária.' *Revista Brasileira de Estudos Pedagogicos* 13 (April/June 1970)

Comparative Education Review 19 (February 1975)

Correa, Héctor. 'Quality of Education and Socioeconomic Development.' *Comparative Education Review* 9 (June 1964): 11–16

Fernandes, Florestan. 'A democratização do ensino.' *Revista Brasileira de Estudos Pedagógicos* 34 (79): 216–225

Fishlow, Albert. 'Brazilian Size Distribution of Income.' *American Economic Review* 62 (1972): 391–402

——. 'Some Reflections on Post-1964 Brazilian Economic Policy.' In *Authoritarian Brazil: Origins, Policies, and Future.* Edited by Alfred Stepan. New Haven: Yale University Press, 1973

Flexa Ribeiro, Carlos. 'A educação no Brasil.' *Jornal do Brasil*, 5 March 1967

Hamburger, Ernest W. 'O exame vestibular e os desajustes do sistema de ensino.' *Educação Hoje*, January/February 1971

Hansen, David O. 'Age Variations in the Formation of Educational and Occupational Career Goals of Brazilian Youth: A Cross-Cultural Test of the Wisconsin Model.' *Comparative Education Review* 21 (February 1977): 32–50

Haussman, Fay. 'Brazil: The Peaceful Revolution.' *Interplay* 4 (March 1971): 15–20

——. 'Brazil's Domestic Peace Corps.' *Saturday Review* (October 9, 1973): 50–51

——. 'Education for Development in Brazil.' *Change* (June 1975): 23–25

Holsinger, Donald B. 'Education and the Occupational Attainment Process in Brazil.' *Comparative Education Review* 19 (June 1975): 267–275

Hutchinson, Bertrand. 'Aspectos da educação universitária e status social em São Paulo.' *Educação e Ciências Sociais* 2 (4): 39–76

Institut International d'Etudes sur l'Education. 'Brazil Plans to Bring Schools into Line with Job Market.' *Bulletin* (August 1971): 2–3

——. 'Brazilian Educators Meet to Reevaluate University Reform.' *Bulletin* (September 1972): 6

——. 'Brazilian Universities Said to be Out of Touch with Lower-level Education.' *Bulletin* (May 1972): 3

——. 'Misión de la Universidad en América Latina.' Brussels: IIEE, 1973

Institute for International Youth Affairs. 'Widespread Violence Shakes Brazil After Policeman Kills Student in Rio.' *News Features* IX (April 25, 1968): 1–2

Kimball, Solon T. 'Primary Education in Brazil.' *Comparative Education Review* 4 (1): 49–54

Langoni, Carlos Geraldo. 'A rentabilidade social dos investimentos em educação no Brasil.' *Ensaios Econômicos*, 1972, pp. 343–378

Leme, Pascoal. 'A educação brasileira num momento crítico.' *Revista Brasileira de Estudos Pedagógicos* 25 (September/October 1959): 95–109

Mascaro, Carlos Corrêa. 'Extensão da Escolaridade.' *Revista Brasileira de Estudos Pedagógicos* 47 (April/June 1967)

Mendes de Almeida, Cândido. 'Sistema político e modêlos de poder no Brasil.' *Dados*, no. 1 (second semester, 1966), pp. 7–15

Myhr, Robert O. 'Student Activism and Development.' In *Contemporary Brazil: Issues in Economic and Political Development.* Edited by H. Jon Rosenbaum and William G. Tyler. New York: Praeger Publishers, 1972

Novitski, Joseph. 'Brazil's Policies Shaped at War College.' *The New York Times*, 2 August 1972

Pastore, José. 'As funções da educação em uma sociedade em mudança.' *Sociologia* 26 (1): 21–31

Poppovic, Ana Maria; Esposito, Yara Lucia; and Campos, Maria Machado Malta. 'Marginalização cultural: subsídios para um currículo pré-escolar.' *Cadernos de Pesquisa*, Fundação Carlos Chagas, No. 14 (September 1975): 7–86

Speller, Paulo. 'La universidad brasileña: un modelo tecnocrático-autoritário de reforma educativa.' *Foro Universitário* 7 (December 1976): 23–29

Toward, Agnes. 'Education: Brazil.' In *Handbook of Latin American Studies*. No. 33. Edited by Donald E. J. Stewart. Gainesville: University of Florida Press, 1971

Waibel, Leo. 'European Colonization in Southern Brazil.' *Geographical Review XL* (October 1950): 529–47

Youth Action, 2 (1971)

Youth and Freedom, 8 (1967)

DOCUMENTS AND REPORTS

Brasil. *Ato Adicional*, 6 August 1834

——. *Constituição da República dos Estados Unidos do Brasil*, 24 February 1891

——. Decreto-lei no. 66.258 de 1970. *Diário Oficial*, 25 February 1971

——. *Ensino Superior, 1973*. Rio de Janeiro: Secretária-Geral, MEC, 1974

——. *Estatísticas da Educação Nacional, 1960–71*. Rio de Janeiro: Secretária-Geral, MEC, 1972

——. *Pesquisa sobre Demanda e Oferta de Vagas no Ensino Superior*. Brasília: Departamento de Assuntos Universitários, Coordenação de Planejamento, MEC, 1973

——. Portaria no. 413, BSB. *Diário Oficial*, 2 June 1972

——. Portaria no. 524, BSB. *Diário Oficial*, 1 September 1971

——. *I Plano Nacional de Desenvolvimento (PND), 1972/74*. Rio de Janeiro: IBGE, 1971

——. *Projeto da Constituição Política do Império do Brasil*, 1 September 1823

——. *Relação entre Ensino de 2° Grau, Formação Profissional e Emprêgo*. Brasília: MEC, 1973

——. *Relatório Anual, 1973*. Brasília: Departamento de Assuntos Universitários, MEC, 1974

——. *II Plano Nacional de Desenvolvimento (1975–1979).* Rio de Janeiro: IBGE, 1974

——. *Sinopse do Ensino Médio, 1972.* Rio de Janeiro: Secretária-Geral, MEC, 1973

Fundação Carlos Chagas. '*Estudo de Algumas Características Sócioculturais de Candidatos ao Ingresso em Escolas de Nivel Superior.*' São Paulo: Fundação Carlos Chagas, 1969

——. *Simpósio sobre Planejamento da Educação.* São Paulo: Fundação Carlos Chagas, 1972

de Carvalho, Guido Ivan. 'Ensino Superior: Legislação e Jurisprudência,' 2ª edição. Rio de Janeiro, 1969

——. 'Ensino Superior: Legislação e Jurisprudência.' 3ª edição. Rio de Janeiro, 1971

——. 'Ensino Superior: Legislação e Jurisprudência.' 4ª edição. Rio de Janeiro, 1973

Castro, Cláudio de Moura. *Eficiência e Custos das Escolas de Nível Médio: Um Estudo-Pilôto na Guanabara.* Relatório de Pesquisa No. 3. Rio de Janeiro: IPEA/NPES, Ministério do Planejamento e Coordenação Geral, 1971

——; Pereira, Milton de Assis; and Furtado, Sandra de Oliveira. *Ensino Técnico: Desempenho e Custos.* Rio de Janeiro: IPEA/INPES, 1972

Fundação CESGRANRIO. *Legislação Atualizada Referente aos Concursos Vestibulares de 1974.* Rio de Janeiro: Fundação CESGRANRIO, 1973

Coelho, Magda Prates, and Pereira, Maria Elisa. *O Emprêgo no Brasil de Profissionais Treinados no Exterior.* Projeto Retorno, Documento no. 4. Rio de Janeiro: Fundação Getúlio Vargas, 1971

Comissão de Ensino Médico. *O Ensino Médico no Brasil.* Brasília: MEC, 1972

Conselho Nacional de Pesquisas. *Projeto SACI: Reunião de Exame de Progresso.* São José dos Campos: Instituto de Pesquisas Espaciais, 1971

Conselho Nacional de Pós-Graduacão. *Plano Nacional de Pós-Graduacão.* Brasília: MEC, 1975

da Cunha, Nádia Franco, ed. *O Acesso à Universidade.* IVª Conferência Nacional de Educação. Rio de Janeiro: INEP, 1967

Departamento Intersindical de Estatística e Estudos Sócio-Econômicos. *Família Assalariada: Padrão e Custo de Vida.* São Paulo: Gráfica da Federação dos Metalurgicos de Sao Paulo, 1974

Dutra, Tarso; dos Reis Velloso, J. P.; Chagas, V.; Sucupira, N.; do Val, F.; Lyra Filho, J.; Moreira Couceiro, A.; Maciel de Barros, R. S.; de Avila, Pe. F.; and Peres, L. *Reforma Universitária.* Brasília: MEC, 1968

Economic Commission for Latin America. *Education, Human Resources and Development.* New York: United Nations, 1968

Economic Commission for Latin America. *Social Change and Development Policy in Latin America.* New York: United Nations, 1970

Escola Superior de Guerra. *Plano Geral de Estudos.* Rio de Janeiro: Escola Superior de Guerra, 1973

Harrell, William A. *Educational Reform in Brazil: The Law of 1961.* Washington, D.C.: U.S. Office of Education, 1968

Instituto Brasileiro de Geografia e Estatística. *Resultados Censitários,* 1970. Rio de Janeiro: IBGE, 1971

Levy, Samuel. *The Demand for Higher-Education and the Labour Market for Professionals in Brazil.* Contract No. AID-12-692. Rio de Janeiro: Human Resources Office, USAID, 1972

Ministério da Educação e Cultura. *Campanha Nacional de Alimentação Escolar: Relatório.* Brasília: MEC, 1973

——. *Caracterização Sócio-Econômica do Estudante Universitário.* Rio de Janeiro: Centro Brasileiro de Pesquisas Educacionais, Instituto Nacional de Estudos Pedagógicos, 1968

——. *Catálogo Geral das Instituições de Ensino Superior: 1973.* Brasília: Departamento de Assuntos Universitários, MEC, 1973

——. *Estatísticas da Educação Nacional, 1971–73.* Brasília: MEC, 1974

——. *Plano de Trabalho de Extensão Universitária.* Brasília: DAU, 1975

Ministério do Interior. *Projeto Rondon: Programas e Metas para 1974.* Brasília: Ministério do Interior, 1973

——. *Relatório da Equipe de Assessoria ao Planejamento do Ensino Superior: Acôrdo MEC-USAID: Rio de Janeiro: MEC, 1969*

Ministério do Exército. *Currículo: Curso de Comando e Estado-Maior a Curso de Chefia e Estado-Maior de Serviço.* Brasília: Departamento de Ensino e Pesquisa. Ministério do Exército, 1972

——. *Plano Geral de Ensino.* Agulhas Negras: Divisão de Ensino, Academia Militar das Agulhas Negras, 1973

Ministério do Planejamento e Coordenação Econômica. *Programa de Ação Econômica do Governo, 1964–66*. Rio de Janeiro: Documentos IPEA, 1964

——. *Programa Estratégico de Desenvolvimento, 1968–1970*. Rio de Janeiro: IBGE, 1967

——. *Sinopse Estatística do Brasil, 1971*. Rio de Janeiro: Fundação IBGE, 1971

Ministry of Education and Culture. *Education in Brazil*. Brasília: Commission for International Affairs, MEC, 1971

——. *Sector Plan for Education and Culture, 1972/1974*. Brasília: General Secretariat, MEC, 1971

Passarinho, Jarbas Gonçalves. *A Educação em Debate*. Brasília: MEC, 1973

——. *Educação Planificada*. Brasília: MEC, 1971

Pastore, José *et al*. *Profissionais Especializados no Mercado de Trabalho*. São Paulo: Instituto de Pesquisas Econômicas, Universidade de São Paulo, 1973

Pereira, Luiz. *O Magistério Primário na Sociedade de Classe*. São Paulo: Faculdade de Filosofia, Ciências e Letras, USP, 1963

Pimenta, Aluísio; dos Santos, Oder José; Guimarães, Magda Soares; and Avelar, Lucia Mercês. *Estabelcimento de uma Politica para Admissão de Alunos no Ensino Superior do Brasil*. Rio de Janeiro: Conselho de Reitores das Universidades Brasileiras, 1967

Ribeiro Netto, Adolpho. *A Fundação Carlos Chagas: Seleção para a Universidade e Pesquisa para a Educação*. São Paulo: Fundação Carlos Chagas, 1973

Sanders, Thomas G. *The Paulo Freire Method: Literacy Training and Conscientización*. Hanover, N. H.: American Universities Field Staff, 1968

Santos, Roberto Figueira. 'Avaliação da Implantação da Reforma Universitária.' *II Encontro de Reitores das Universidades Públicas e Diretores de Estabelecimentos Públicos Isolados de Ensino Superior*. Brasília: Ministério da Educação e Cultura, 1973

Serpa, Carlos Alberto. *Simpósio para Avaliação de Reforma nas Universidades Brasileiras: Concurso Vestibular*. Rio de Janeiro: Pontifícia Universidade Católica do Rio de Janeiro, 1971

United Nations, ed. *Access to Higher Education* Vol. 2. Liège, Belgium: United Nations Educational, Scientific and Cultural Organization and the International Association of Universities, 1965

——. *Demographic Yearbook*, 1970. 1971

——. *Demographic Yearbook*, 1972. 1973

United Nations Educational, Scientific and Cultural Organization. *Statistical Yearbook*, 1970. 1971

——. *Statistical Yearbook*, 1972. 1973

U.S., Agency for International Development. *Brazil: Education Sector Analysis*. Rio de Janeiro: Human Resources Office, USAID, 1972

Universidade Federal da Bahia. *Avaliação da Implantação da Reforma Universitária*. Volume I. Salvador: Emprêsa Gráfica da Bahia, 1975

UNPUBLISHED MATERIALS

Sander, Benno. 'Educational Law and Practice in a Developing Country: An Empirical Study of the Impact Made by Brazilian Law No. 4024 on Secondary Education in the State of Rio Grande do Sul.' Ph.D. dissertation, Catholic University of America, 1970

Senna, José Julio de Almeida. 'Schooling, Job Experience and Earnings in Brazil.' Ph.D. dissertation, Johns Hopkins University, 1975

Toward, Agnes. 'Some Aspects of the Federal Education Council in the Brazilian Education System.' Ph.D. dissertation, University of Texas, 1966

Index

LIBRARY ... LEGE